Unveiling the Magic of Christmas Cookies

Seasonal Sweets Unveiled: An Introduction to Christmas Cookies

Daniel Mitchell

© Copyright 2023 - All rights reserved.

The content contained within this book may not be reproduced, duplicated or transmitted without direct written permission from the author or the publisher.

Under no circumstances will any blame or legal responsibility be held against the publisher, or author, for any damages, reparation, or monetary loss due to the information contained within this book, either directly or indirectly.

Legal Notice:

This book is copyright protected. It is only for personal use. You cannot amend, distribute, sell, use, quote or paraphrase any part, or the content within this book, without the consent of the author or publisher.

Disclaimer Notice:

Please note the information contained within this document is for educational and entertainment purposes only. All effort has been executed to present accurate, up to date, reliable, complete information. No warranties of any kind are declared or implied. Readers acknowledge that the author is not engaging in the rendering of legal, financial, medical or professional advice. The content within this book has been derived from various sources. Please consult a licensed professional before attempting any techniques outlined in this book.

By reading this document, the reader agrees that under no circumstances is the author responsible for any losses, direct or indirect, that are incurred as a result of the use of information contained within this document, including, but not limited to, errors, omissions, or inaccuracies.

Table of Contents

INTRODUCTION 5

CHAPTER I: The Art of Baking 7

    Essential Baking Tools and Ingredients 7

    Mastering Basic Cookie Dough 10

    Tips and Tricks for Perfect Christmas Cookie Texture ... 14

CHAPTER II: Classic Christmas Cookie Recipes 19

    Sugar Cookies: A Blank Canvas for Creativity 19

    Gingerbread Cookies: A Holiday Staple 23

    Snickerdoodles: Cinnamon Perfection 27

    Peppermint Meltaways: Refreshing Holiday Delight 30

CHAPTER III: Beyond the Basics 34

    Stained Glass Cookies: Edible Decorations.................... 34

    Linzer Cookies: Elegant and Jam-Filled......................... 37

    Thumbprint Cookies: Personalized Treats 41

CHAPTER IV: Gluten-Free and Vegan Options 46

    Almond Flour Sugar Cookies: Gluten-Free Bliss 46

    Vegan Gingerbread Stars: Cruelty-Free Festivity 49

    Tips for Adapting Recipes to Special Dietary Needs 53

CHAPTER V: Cookie Decorating Techniques 58

    Royal Icing Basics: From Flood to Flow 58

    Piping and Flooding: Creating Intricate Designs 62

    Edible Paints and Glazes: Unleashing Your Artistic Side 66

CHAPTER VI: Gift-Giving and Packaging Ideas 72

    Creating Cookie Gift Boxes: A Thoughtful Gesture 72

    Packaging Tips for Freshness and Presentation 76

    Homemade Tags and Labels: Adding a Personal Touch 80

CHAPTER VII: Cookie Exchange Parties 85

    Hosting a Successful Cookie Swap 85

    Unique Themes for a Memorable Event 89

    Recipes Ideal for Cookie Exchange Parties 93

CHAPTER VIII: Christmas Cookie Traditions Around the World 98

    Italian Pizzelles: Anise-Flavored Delight 98

    German Lebkuchen: Spiced and Iced Perfection 102

    Mexican Wedding Cookies: A Festive Treat 106

CHAPTER IX: Troubleshooting and FAQs 110

    Common Cookie Baking Problems and Solutions 110

    Frequently Asked Questions About Christmas Cookies 113

CONCLUSION 119

INTRODUCTION

Here, you may discover the magical realm of "Unveiling the Magic of Christmas Cookies: Seasonal Sweets Unveiled – An Introduction to Christmas Cookies." There's a distinct feeling of excitement and expectation in the air as the holidays get near, and houses smell deliciously of freshly made cookies. The art of baking and enjoying Christmas cookies is a beloved tradition, and it is celebrated in this e-book.

We travel beyond the traditional recipes in these pages, exploring the delightful anecdotes, cultural importance, and creative inventiveness associated with Christmas cookies. This electronic book is intended to be your all-in-one resource, providing the ideal balance of background information, methods, and innovative ideas to enhance your holiday baking endeavors.

We'll go over the foundations of baking in detail in each chapter, covering everything from making the basic cookie dough to the delicate decorating technique. There's something for everyone, regardless of expertise level, as we dissect traditional recipes, find inventive adaptations, and even go into gluten-free and vegan choices.

But there's more to this e-book than just a bunch of recipes. It's an invitation to bring the enchantment of Christmas cookies into your holiday celebration. We'll walk you through the customs that make this time of year so unique, from the delight of presenting elegantly wrapped cookie presents to organizing exciting cookie exchange events.

Explore the diverse range of Christmas cookie customs around the globe, encompassing Italian and German Lebkuchen, and discover how these delightful pastries hold a special place in many festivals.

Every dish and tale inspires you, sparks your imagination, and adds enchantment as you flip the pages. Cheers to a season full of coziness, good times, and the seductive charm of Christmas sweets!

CHAPTER I

The Art of Baking

Essential Baking Tools and Ingredients

A collection of essential equipment and materials is required to unlock the full potential of baking, sometimes referred to as the alchemical skill of changing simple elements into delightful masterpieces. When baking, having the correct tools and being precise are two of the most important factors determining success. Our exploration of the world of vital baking tools and ingredients has led us to realize that a well-equipped kitchen serves as the canvas upon which the magic of baking is revealed.

Every baker should have a collection of measuring equipment since they are the foundation of accuracy. When it comes to baking, having precise measurements is essential, as even a minute variance can throw off the delicate equilibrium of the components and put the

quality
of the result up for debate. To ensure that flour, sugar, and other components are combined harmonically, it is essential to have measuring cups and spoons, graded mixing bowls, and a dependable kitchen scale.

When mixing, which is combining components into a cohesive batter or dough, having the appropriate set of instruments is essential. When it comes to managing dense bread dough or light cake mixes, a stand mixer, with its adaptable attachments, is the tool that simplifies the process and offers the required muscle. An ergonomic spatula and a robust whisk become extensions of the baker's hands, promoting a tactile connection with the ingredients. This is especially beneficial for those individuals who prefer a hands-on approach.

Accurate temperature management is essential for the oven, which is the most sacred space in the baking process. A trustworthy oven thermometer becomes a caretaker of accuracy when it comes to ensuring that delicate pastries rise and beautiful brown crusts develop at the ideal temperature. To prevent sticking and ensure that heat is distributed evenly, baking sheets, parchment paper, and silicone mats serve as the canvas onto which the masterpieces are formed.

Both baking powder and baking soda are considered unsung heroes in the world of leavening agents. When activated by heat or acid, these seemingly little granules produce the chemical reactions that drive dough to rise and attain the desired texture. Yeast, a living microbe, takes This process one step further. Within bread and other yeast-based compositions, yeast introduces a complex interplay of fermentation and taste development.

There are many different varieties of flour, each of which contributes a unique set of properties to the finished product. Flour is the essential component that is used to construct the majority of baked items. One of the most adaptable options for various dishes is all-purpose flour, which has a well-balanced protein level. Specialty flours such as almond, coconut, or gluten-free alternatives cater to specific dietary choices, while whole wheat flour imparts a nutty taste and a substantial texture to the ingredient.

Not only can sweeteners, such as granulated and brown sugar, honey, and maple syrup, contribute to the sweetness of baked goods, but they also possess the ability to affect the moisture content, color, and texture of these products. A significant contribution to the texture and flavor profile of the finished product is made by fats, which include butter, oil, and shortening. These fats give richness and moisture to the process.

In baking, eggs are a multipurpose powerhouse due to their exceptional capacity to emulsify, leaven, and bind materials. Their flexibility as a foundational component is demonstrated by their lending structure to cakes, stability to custards, and delectability to cookies. Baked foods receive an increase in moisture, softness, and taste complexity when dairy products such as milk, cream, and yogurt are included.

To enhance the sensory experience of baking, flavor extracts, spices, and zest are all essential ingredients. Many different recipes benefit from using vanilla extract, one of the most common flavorings. It gives the dish a sense of depth and warmth. Citrus zest imparts brightness and a burst of freshness, while cinnamon, nutmeg, and other spices contribute to the fragrant richness of the dish.

When it comes to baking in the current day, inventiveness has no limits, and a plethora of specialized instruments have recently appeared to appeal to a wide variety of preferences and tastes. Techniques like cookie cutters, pastry bags, and tips make creating elaborate shapes and artistic flourishes possible. Rolling pins, dough scrapers, and bench knives are all helpful tools when shaping and working with different types of dough. Pans considered specialty pans, such as tart pans and bundt pans, provide the finished product with distinctive forms and textures.

We are about to begin a journey beyond the technical aspects of baking as we prepare ourselves with these required instruments and components. Each measurement, each fold of dough, and each time spent in the oven plays a part in developing something more than the sum of its parts. Precision becomes an art at this point. An alchemical change takes place in the hands of the baker, transforming raw components into a symphony of tastes, textures, and smells. This transition is the essence of baking, not just the equipment and ingredients involved. A laboratory is created in the kitchen due to the dance between science and art, and the baker, a culinary alchemist, creates magic in the shape of delectable and luxurious sweets.

Mastering Basic Cookie Dough

Mastering the skill of basic cookie dough is one of the few activities in baking that is both financially profitable and adaptable. A cookie dough that has been carefully created may serve as the basis for an infinite variety of delectable sweets, ranging from the traditional simplicity of sugar cookies to the reassuring richness of chocolate chips and everything in between. This essay aims to go into the fundamental aspects of mastering basic cookie dough. It will investigate the intricacies of the components, the science of mixing, and the art of attaining that exact balance that results in cookies with the appropriate texture, flavor, and look.

A fundamental cookie dough is a straightforward mixture of flour, sugar, fat, leavening agents, and flavorings. This is the essence of every cookie dough. However, the secret to success rests in the amounts of these elements and the order in which they are combined inside the recipe. The development of gluten, which occurs when flour is mixed with wet substances, gives cookie dough its structure. Flour is the foundation of most cookie doughs. An excessive amount of flour might result in dry and crumbly cookies, while insufficient flour can prevent a dough from spreading excessively while baked. It is essential to strike the correct balance.

There is a significant impact on the final product's texture and flavor that may be attributed to the selection of fat. In many traditional cookie recipes, butter is a favored ingredient because of its savory flavor and its capacity to facilitate spreading. Shortening, on the other hand, is an excellent option for specific applications since it helps keep the cookie's form while also contributing to creating a sensitive crumb. To achieve a harmonious equilibrium between flavor and structure, several recipes combine both types of fats.

Not only does sugar have the ability to sweeten, but it also affects the texture, color, and moisture retention of cookies. Brown sugar adds moisture and a hint of molasses, which results in a chewier texture, while granulated sugar contributes to a crisp surface. Granulated sugar is responsible for the crispy outside. The finished cookie's personality is partially determined by the proportion of sugars to fat, the method in which the sugars are creamed, and the fat during the mixing process.

The chemical catalysts that allow cookies to rise via baking are known as leavening agents. Examples of leavening agents include baking powder and baking soda. On the other hand, baking soda depends on the acidity in the dough to activate its leavening activity. In contrast, baking powder offers lift by releasing carbon dioxide when it is allowed to be heated. When getting the proper thickness and texture in the completed cookie, having a solid understanding of these agents' roles is necessary.

The cookie's structure and suppleness are strengthened by the addition of eggs, which act as a binding and emulsifying agent. The consistency of the dough is affected not only by the amount of eggs but also by the size of those eggs. An excessive amount of eggs might produce a texture similar to that of cake, while an insufficient amount can result in a cookie that is crumbly or dry. Extracts and flavorings, such as vanilla or almond extract, give the cookie its final touch. They elevate the cookie's taste profile and provide depth to the scent of the cookie.

When it comes to baking, the mixing step is where the science and the art of baking meet. Overmixing can result in the creation of an excessive amount of gluten, which can cause cookies to become challenging. Alternatively, undermixing can result in pockets of unmixed components, which can disrupt the consistency of the flavor and texture of the final product. One of the most distinguishing characteristics of an experienced baker is the ability to strike a delicate balance between complete integration and restraint.

One of the most fundamental steps in preparing many cookie recipes is the traditional creaming process, which involves beating together sugar and butter to include air. In addition to contributing to the cookie's delicate and soft texture, this aeration helps the biscuit to rise while it is baking. It is essential to determine the sequence in which components are added, and a systematic approach guarantees that flavors and leavening agents are distributed evenly throughout the mixture.

Chilling the dough before adding it to the oven is an essential one that is sometimes skipped. It helps solidify the fat, preventing it from spreading too much and enables the flour to hydrate properly, improving the dough's flavor and texture. When it comes to the final product, this resting period, whether in the refrigerator or the freezer, is a minor investment that yields significant returns.

The last factors in the equation of cookie mastery are the baking temperature and the amount of time spent baking. The texture of the cookie is determined by the duration of the baking process, which can range from soft and chewy to crisp and golden. A precise oven temperature ensures that the cookies bake evenly. One factor contributing to the right balance between gooey and set cookies is understanding when to remove them from the oven and allow them to finish cooking on the hot baking sheet.

Getting a handle on basic cookie dough requires an understanding of science and an openness to creativity. This basic dough may be a canvas for various variants, such as incorporating chocolate chips and nuts, experimenting with other extracts and spices, etc. An infinite number of alternatives enables bakers to fashion their masterpieces according to their individual preferences and the inspirations of the season.

To summarize, reaching mastery over basic cookie dough is an investigation into the complex relationship between science and art. It is necessary to grasp the specific function of each component, the chemistry of mixing, and the influence of the factors involved in baking. On the other hand, it is also a call to innovation, encouraging bakers to incorporate their unique sense of individuality into each batch. As the kitchen is filled with the enticing scent of freshly made cookies, it becomes a monument to the expertise that has been accomplished. Every delectable mouthful is a perfect combination of accuracy and passion, science and creativity.

Tips and Tricks for Perfect Christmas Cookie Texture

Achieving the ideal texture in Christmas cookies is an art that requires a combination of accuracy, expertise, and a dash of enchantment that is reminiscent of the holiday season. It is not enough to describe the mouthfeel of a cookie; the texture of a cookie is the result of a complex dance between the ingredients, the mixing procedures, and the baking methods, which ultimately results in a pleasurable sensory experience. The purpose of this essay is to examine a collection of suggestions and techniques designed to assist bakers in achieving the ambitious objective of producing Christmas cookies that have a texture that is, to put it simply, exquisite.

Selecting the appropriate flour is one of the most important factors to consider when creating the optimal texture. One of the most critical factors determining the cookie's structure and softness is the type of flour used. Because it contains a modest amount of protein, all-purpose flour is a versatile option used in various recipes for a balanced texture. Cake flour may be the critical ingredient for individuals looking for a more delicate and sensitive finish. Bread flour, on the other hand, is an excellent choice for cookies that require a chewier texture because of the more significant amount of protein that flour contains.

It is of the utmost necessity to comprehend the significance of accurate measurement to accomplish the desired texture. An excessive amount of flour can cause cookies to be thick and dry, while an insufficient amount might cause desserts to be too soft and spread out. To ensure that the measurements are exact and constant, using measuring cups created exclusively for dry ingredients is recommended. It is possible to avoid compaction and ensure accuracy by spooning flour into the cup and then leveling it off with a flat edge. This will set the scene for a cookie that has a texture that is pleasing to the touch.

Cookie texture is mainly determined by the amount of lipids, particularly butter, that are used in the recipe. One of the most important factors to consider is the butter's temperature at the beginning of the mixing procedure. It is common practice to use butter that has been softened and is at room temperature when creaming sugar to generate a light and airy texture. On the other hand, cold butter is appropriate for use in cookies made using the creaming method to provide structure and leavening. The decision between these two methods might significantly influence the texture of the cookie produced.

The careful assessment of the amount of sugar present is another component contributing to achieving the ideal texture. Granulated sugar is responsible for the crispness of the surface of a cookie. In contrast, brown sugar adds moisture, chewiness, and molasses flavor to the cookie throughout the baking process. Adjustments can be made to the ratio and kind of sugars and the manner of creaming with the fat to create the right balance between chewy and crunchy textures.

Baking powder and baking soda are two examples of leavening chemicals that add a layer of complication to achieving the ideal cookie texture. As a result of its contribution to a light and fluffy texture, baking powder is well-suited for use in cakes and cookies that are more tender. As a result of the acidity in the dough, baking soda is activated, which helps with spreading and can result in a crispier texture. By gaining an understanding of the intricacies of these leavening agents, bakers are providing themselves with the ability to adjust their recipes to create the specific texture they envisage.

When it comes to texture, the mixing process is where the real alchemy takes place. Overmixing can lead to an excessive formation of gluten, which might result in cookies that are difficult to chew. To prevent this from happening, it is necessary to mix the ingredients until they are completely incorporated, which will result in a soft crumb. It is common practice to favor minimum mixing when making cookies that demand a more delicate touch, such as shortbread. This allows the dough to keep its crumbly, melt-in-the-mouth quality.

Putting the cookie dough in the refrigerator before baking is a standard method used to control the spread and improve the texture of the cookies. During this process, the fats are solidified, preventing the cookies from spreading out too thinly when baked. Additionally, it enables the flour to hydrate thoroughly, resulting in a more cohesive and tasty dough. The amount of time required to chill the ingredients might vary depending on the recipe and the desired outcome; nonetheless, this step that requires patience is a relatively minor investment that yields significant benefits in terms of texture.

Further refining the texture of Christmas cookies may be accomplished by experimenting with different egg ratios. Eggs are a source of moisture, structure, and richness; the composition of the texture may be tailored to particular requirements by varying the number of eggs used. A more excellent egg ratio often produces a texture similar to cake, but a lower egg ratio can have a crumbly or sandy texture. The ability to intentionally manipulate the final texture is made possible by understanding the role of eggs in the recipe.

Cookies receive an increase in taste and the complexity of their texture when mix-ins like chocolate chips, almonds, or dried fruits are incorporated into the recipe. Both the size and the kind of mix-ins can affect the overall mouthfeel. Larger chunks can provide pockets of gooey pleasure, while smaller bits can contribute to a more uniform distribution of taste and texture. The challenge is striking a balance between these additions so that they complement rather than dominate the natural texture of the cookie.

The texture is ultimately determined by the time spent baking and the temperature. It is necessary to thoroughly comprehend the intended outcome to adhere to the golden rule of baking, which is to know when to remove cookies from the oven. A shorter baking period often results in cookies that are chewier and softer, while a lengthier duration brings about cookies that have a crispier texture. A factor contributing to the final set of cookies is the residual heat left on the baking sheet after removing the oven. This is a component that adds subtlety to the texture.

The skill of creating the correct texture in Christmas cookies is a dynamic interaction of ingredients, processes, and personal tastes. This is the case, particularly in the area of Christmas cookies. The method of achieving cookie excellence requires first gaining a grasp of the function of each component and then being proficient in the procedures that harmonize them. The beauty of the method is in the latitude for creativity and experimentation that it provides. This allows bakers to modify their recipes to cater to the tastes of individuals they wish to delight in terms of texture. Each flavor is a tribute to the meticulous deliberation and creativity put into making the right texture, which is the trademark of a seasoned and discriminating baker. As the scent of freshly made Christmas cookies fills the air, each bite becomes a monument to the perfect texture.

CHAPTER II

Classic Christmas Cookie Recipes

Sugar Cookies: A Blank Canvas for Creativity

Sugar cookies are one of the few delectable treats that exemplify the spirit of artistic expression in such a profound way within the broad field of baking. Sugar cookies, which are uncomplicated in their structure but may be used in unlimited ways, are like a blank canvas ready to be painted on by the artist's imagination. These traditional sweets are more than just confections; they are an invitation to explore design, flavor, and creative expression in the comfort of one's kitchen. The magical world of sugar cookies is investigated in this article. The fundamental components of sugar cookies, the skill of decorating them, and the numerous ways these mouthwatering canvases may be converted into culinary masterpieces are all covered.

The simplicity of the sugar cookie's composition, which is also harmonic, is the source of its endearing qualities. The combination of flour, butter, sugar, eggs, and a dash of vanilla extract results in a dough that is not only soft but also robust. Creating a softly sweet cookie that serves as the appropriate basis for a wide variety of tastes and artistic decorations is made possible by the simplicity of the ingredients, which allows for a delicate balance to be achieved.

The dough itself, which has a neutral taste profile, serves as a blank canvas ready to absorb and display the essence of various extracts, spices, and add-ins. Sugar cookie dough is a flexible basis that may be used to create a wide variety of flavor combinations, ranging from the traditional appeal of vanilla to the warmth of almond or the zest of citrus. Because of this plasticity, bakers can alter their products to reflect seasonal inspirations or thematic festivities, in addition to catering to the tastes of individual customers.

During the decorating process, the sugar cookie artwork is brought to life in a way that is simply remarkable. Sugar cookies have a smooth, flat surface that provides a lot of opportunity for creative designs and delicate features to be included in the biscuit. When decorating sugar cookies, royal icing is a time-honored option that acts as the artist's medium. It provides a smooth and glossy texture that is ideal for providing a backdrop for intricate patterns and brilliant colors. There are a variety of effects that may be achieved by adjusting the consistency of the icing. These effects range from a flood, which creates seamless backdrops, to thicker consistencies, which need precise contours and decorations.

To turn sugar cookie dough into edible works of art, cookie cutters are being utilized in an infinite variety of forms and sizes. The only thing that may restrict the options is the baker's imagination. The choices range from typical holiday patterns like snowflakes and Christmas trees to funny forms such as animals, letters, and even unique designs. The process of selecting and utilizing cookie cutters is more than just a matter of shape; it also entails telling stories, communicating ideas, and evoking feelings via the visual language of cookies.

It is common practice for decorating cookies to comprise a series of phases, beginning with the outline and continuing with the flooding of the cookie with base colors. After being allowed to cure, royal icing produces a smooth surface that may be used as a canvas for further decorating layers. Creating texture, depth, and visual interest may be accomplished with various piping methods, including flooding, piping, and marbling, which offer a range of options. Additional dimensions are added to the artwork using edible markers, food gels, and luster
dust. These materials create delicate details, shading, and a touch of glitter.

In addition to the conventional royal icing, there are other techniques of decorating sugar cookies that accommodate a wide range of preferences and skill levels. Cookies may be finished with a smooth and polished appearance by rolling out fondant, a malleable sugar paste that can be draped over cookies. It functions as a flexible medium that can sculpt elaborate designs, create three-dimensional elements, and achieve a faultless look that is worthy of being shown in a bakery.

Sanding sugars, sprinkles, and edible glitter is a quick and fun way to add flare to sugar cookies. This is especially useful for individuals looking for a more casual approach to decorating. It is possible to apply these straightforward decorations either before baking or after frosting, and they will add a touch of sweetness, texture, and color to the finished product. The fact that these embellishments are appealing to the senses (both tactile and sensory) provides an additional dimension of pleasure to the experience of eating cookies.

When it comes to a variety of ethnic and seasonal rituals, sugar cookies are also at the heart of the action. Baking and decorating sugar cookies is a Christmas tradition highly valued in many households. This activity brings together families and friends in a shared creative endeavor, which is a valuable experience for everyone involved. During the holiday season, rolling out the dough, cutting shapes, and decorating cookies with festive designs becomes a joyous pastime, fostering a sense of joy and camaraderie among the participants.

Not only do sugar cookies have a visually appealing appearance, but they also play an essential function in distributing gifts and festivities. When it comes to birthdays, marriages, and other special events, sugar cookies that have been decorated make for beautiful and unique presents that provide a touch of heart to the recipient. As edible gifts of gratitude, personalized cookie favors designed to match an event's theme serve as a unique and memorable addition to festivities while also serving as a gesture of appreciation.

There is no limit to the creativity that can be applied to sugar cookies. The proliferation of cookie decorating seminars, online tutorials, and social media platforms devoted explicitly to cookie artistry has resulted in a thriving community of bakers eager to share their expertise, ideas, and accomplishments. In addition to being a culinary activity, sugar cookie decorating has evolved into a collaborative art due to sharing skills, celebrating achievements, and encouraging in the face of problems.

In our exploration into sugar cookies, we realize that these sweet treats are more than just a simple indulgence; instead, they celebrate creativity, uniqueness, and the pleasure of sharing edible art. Not only do sugar cookies have a pleasant flavor, but they also impart a transformational power that makes them appealing to bakers of all skill levels. This is what makes sugar cookies so appealing. Whether you are a rookie decorator or an experienced artist, each sugar cookie becomes a one-of-a-kind expression of inspiration and imagination. This transforms a simple delicacy into a mouthwatering masterpiece that captivates the eyes and tantalizes the taste buds. Cookies made of sugar transcend their simple beginnings to become a medium for edible art when they are in the hands of a baker enthusiastic about baking. They are a delectable celebration of creativity and the sweetness of life.

Gingerbread Cookies: A Holiday Staple

Few baked goods have the same sentimental appeal and celebratory importance as gingerbread cookies during Christmas. These spiced treats are a wintertime mainstay, decorating tables, tree branches, and cookie platters with their distinct flavor and cozy scent. Gingerbread cookies are not just a delicious treat; they symbolize a culture rich in custom and festive mood. This article explores the lengthy history, unique components, and creative adaptations that make gingerbread cookies a cherished and enduring Christmas mainstay.

Gingerbread has a long and rich history with many different cultures and customs. Ginger has been used in baking since medieval Europe when people prized the spice for its unique flavor and alleged therapeutic benefits. At first, gingerbread was a pricey confection favored by the nobility; it was decorated with elaborate designs and gold leaf. Gingerbread made its way into European kitchens as trade routes grew, making spices like ginger more widely available.

It is said that Queen Elizabeth I popularized the practice of adorning gingerbread figurines as presents in the sixteenth century. These ornately decorated gingerbread sculptures evolved to represent kindness and welcome. As the custom of sculpting gingerbread into human and animal forms grew in popularity, gingerbread men, women, and even entire villages were made. The festive scent and endearing forms have come to be associated with Christmas.

Gingerbread cookies' unique flavor and texture result from its basic components. An essential ingredient, molasses, not only gives the dough a rich, dark color but also a subtle bitterness that counteracts the sweetness of the sugar. Brown sugar adds moisture and a chewy texture to the taste profile and balances it with its molasses content. The main attraction, ground ginger, provides the distinct warmth and spice that make gingerbread unique. These cookies are a seasonal favorite because of their rich and fragrant flavor, enhanced by additional spices like nutmeg, cloves, and cinnamon.

With its aromatic spice combination, gingerbread dough is an excellent medium for artistic expression. Whether they are classic figures or modern patterns, rolling out and cutting gingerbread forms adds a fun, hands-on aspect to baking. A sense of artistry is evoked by the accuracy needed to cut out forms, transforming each cookie into a tiny piece of artwork. The baking releases a delicious perfume into the kitchen, reminding me of family get-togethers and the exuberant build-up to celebrations.

Through decorating techniques, gingerbread cookies provide a canvas for more artistic expression. With its glossy, smooth texture, royal icing is a standard option for adorning gingerbread creations with elaborate decorations and brilliant colors. The adaptability of royal icing allows for a range of options, from basic contours to intricate patterns, transforming each gingerbread figure into a distinctive and eye-catching masterpiece. The visual appeal of these festive delights is enhanced by adding texture and glitter provided by nonpareils, dragees, and colored sugars.

Gingerbread homes have transcended typical forms and have come to represent the exquisite artistry of the Christmas season. The essential gingerbread cookie is transformed into a fanciful and delectable architectural marvel when assembled into tiny houses decorated with frosting and various sweets. Decorating gingerbread houses has become a beloved family tradition that encourages cooperation and creativity as each member builds and decorates the confection.

Gingerbread cookies are a Christmas favorite now essential to many cultures' traditions and festivities. Christmas markets in Germany, the birthplace of many gingerbread customs, are known for their elaborate Lebkuchen pastries. Pepparkakor cookies are a favorite in Sweden; they are frequently fashioned into hearts and stars and put as decorations on Christmas trees. In the US, gingerbread cookies are not only eaten at home but also have a big part in the customs of competitions, festivities, and gingerbread house displays.

Gingerbread has more meaning than just its delicious flavor and festive look. Gingerbread cookies frequently have sentimental significance because they evoke memories of family customs, holiday gatherings, and the delight of giving and receiving tasty presents. Making gingerbread becomes a social activity that unites people to partake in producing and consuming these classic sweets. The spices' warmth enhances gingerbread's emotional resonance during the Christmas season, as well as the sweetness of the molasses and the artistic embellishments.

In addition to being delicious and fragrant, gingerbread cookies serve as a vehicle for cultural expression. Gingerbread figurines' designs and forms frequently capture local and familial influences. The variety of gingerbread patterns, which range from traditional men and women to imaginative renditions with animals, trees, and snowflakes, reflects the variety of seasonal rituals and traditions. A treasured method of maintaining a cultural legacy and honoring the continuation of family customs is passing along gingerbread recipes and skills from one generation to the next.

The popularity of gingerbread has spread to other culinary and creative fields in recent years, beyond only the kitchen. Desserts with gingerbread flavors, like ice cream and lattes, have become seasonal favorites. The talent for creating beautiful and inventive gingerbread masterpieces has been showcased by professional and amateur bakers alike in elaborate exhibitions and contests that have emerged from the art of gingerbread sculpting. The timeless appeal of gingerbread comes from its capacity to inspire and adapt to new and inventive culinary creations in addition to its time-tested recipes.

In conclusion, gingerbread cookies are a beloved and classic Christmas mainstay, capturing the essence of custom, inventiveness, and joy. Gingerbread has been ingrained in the traditions of holiday celebrations, from its modest beginnings as spiced snacks in medieval times to the intricate gingerbread houses and sculpted marvels of today. Gingerbread decoration and baking became a pleasant creative expression and a means of preserving cultural and family customs. During the Christmas season, the scent of gingerbread, which is both sweet and spicy, permeates homes, reminding people of the cheer and warmth that this popular food provides to people all over the world.

Snickerdoodles: Cinnamon Perfection

Snickerdoodles are one of the cookies that capture the cozy feel of making at home. Cookie lovers have a particular place in their hearts for Snickerdoodles because of their crackly exterior, soft inside, and distinctive cinnamon-sugar coating. These understated yet incredibly delicious treats prove alchemy's potency and the straightforward blending of components. This article explores the allure, background, and creative simplicity that contribute to the enduring popularity of Snickerdoodles—a treat known for its impeccable cinnamon flavor.

The Snickerdoodle's charm lies in its uncomplicated yet tasteful blend of common ingredients. A balance of flour, butter, sugar, eggs, baking soda, and cream of tartar comes together to make cookie dough. The unusual acidic component known as cream of tartar gives snickerdoodles their particular texture and their signature tang. When the ingredients are combined and weighed out correctly, the outcome is a delicate and chewy cookie with a hint of tanginess that sets it apart from the norm.

Cream of tartar's function in the leavening process is one characteristic that makes snickerdoodles unique. Snickerdoodles use cream of tartar, which causes a chemical reaction that releases carbon dioxide, unlike other cookies that use baking soda. This process called the creaming of tartar, gives the cookies their distinct chewiness and helps them rise during baking. Snickerdoodles are unique among cookies because of the unique blend of baking soda and cream of tartar, which also gives them a particular flavor and texture.

The main character, cinnamon, is present in every facet of the Snickerdoodle experience. The cookie batter contains ground cinnamon, which gives each mouthful the full flavor of the spice. But the magic doesn't stop there. The pleasant tradition of rolling the cookie dough balls in a combination of sugar and cinnamon before baking makes snickerdoodles unique. This coating gives the Snickerdoodle its distinctively crackly appearance and adds another layer of taste.

More than just a cooking technique, rolling snickerdoodle dough in cinnamon sugar is an artistic process that involves the baker's whole body and involves them in the making of each cookie. The ritual created by the warm dough, the delightful scent of cinnamon, and the baking texture of the sugar crystals turn baking into a happy and cozy pastime. It's a time to engage directly with the ingredients, honor the ageless delight of handcrafted sweets, and celebrate simplicity.

Beyond just their ingredient list, Snickerdoodles' unique look also contributes to their simplicity. Each cookie has a rustic and welcoming charm due to its crackly surface, a product of the leavening process, and the cinnamon-sugar coating. The cookies frequently have a golden-brown, crinkled outside that gives away the soft, chewy within. The visual attractiveness of snickerdoodles enhances their total sensory enjoyment, as does the perfume of sweet and spicy spices wafting through the kitchen while they bake.

Snickerdoodles have their cultural origins in the baking customs of Germany and the Netherlands. The precise meaning of the name "snickerdoodle" is obscured by legend; hypotheses range from a playful wordplay to a reference to the standard German phrase "schneckennudeln," which refers to sweet buns coated with cinnamon. Notwithstanding its name's ambiguity, Snickerdoodles became well-known and a mainstay in American home kitchens. Their popularity around the holidays and ease of preparation made them a popular option for both bakers and families.

Snickerdoodles are versatile since they may be made in various ways and are suitable for multiple settings. Though the traditional recipe is a favorite, creative bakers have experimented with many takes on the snickerdoodle motif. Some versions add layers of taste and texture to the dough using ingredients like chocolate chips, almonds, or dried fruit. Others can go around with other sugar coatings, adding spices like nutmeg or cardamom for a distinctive take on the classic cinnamon-sugar combination.

The fact that Snickerdoodle bars, cupcakes, and even ice cream with a Snickerdoodle taste are still in demand is proof of their continuing appeal. Beyond its classic shape, the essence of Snickerdoodle taste has inspired a variety of delicious concoctions that honor the cozy pairing of sugar and cinnamon. These variants highlight the classic appeal of snickerdoodles as a taste profile that works well with a wide range of culinary ideas.

Sharing Snickerdoodles becomes more than just a fun way to eat the cookies—it's also a way to show love and hospitality. Snickerdoodles are a great gift option on holidays, birthdays, or any other occasion when a little handmade sweetness is appreciated because of their pleasant simplicity. Snickerdoodles, when presented in adorable cookie tins or tied with colorful ribbons, arouse feelings of nostalgia and send a sincere message of love and friendship.

Even in this day of gourmet cuisine and intricate desserts, the timeless attraction of simplicity is demonstrated by Snickerdoodles. They serve as a reminder that a delight that captivates the senses and warms the heart may be made with a few staple ingredients prepared with care and effort. Snickerdoodles' understated attractiveness comes from their capacity to arouse feelings of coziness, bring back fond childhood memories, and celebrate the beauty of simple pleasures rather than from their opulence or complexity. Every time a Snickerdoodle comes out of the oven with its crisp surface and cozy cinnamon scent, it serves as a reminder of the eternal happiness that may be found in the straightforward satisfaction of a skillfully made cookie.

Peppermint Meltaways: Refreshing Holiday Delight

Few sweets among the festive array of Christmas favorites capture the season's spirit quite like Peppermint Meltaways. The decadent, buttery richness of shortbread and peppermint's cold, refreshing flavor combine perfectly in these delicate, melt-in-your-mouth biscuits. Peppermint Meltaways, with their powdered sugar covering resembling snow and a subtle peppermint flavor, have become a beloved wintertime favorite. This essay explores the background, the creative formulation, and the enjoyable taste of Peppermint Meltaways, which make them a delightfully refreshing Christmas treat.

The narrative of Peppermint Meltaways is one of culinary alchemy, in which a few essential ingredients are combined to create a delightful dessert that perfectly embodies the spirit of the holidays. The main ingredients of Peppermint Meltaways cookie dough are flour, butter, powdered sugar, and a small amount of cornstarch. These melt-in-your-mouth cookies have a delicate, crumbly texture enhanced by cornstarch. Consequently, the dish is a picture of simplicity that highlights the creamy, buttery base and lets the peppermint taste come through.

The main component, peppermint, gives the cookies a unique, energizing aroma. The peppermint taste, usually added as finely crushed candy canes or peppermint essence, creates an excellent contrast to the sweetness of the powdered sugar coating. The peppermint's fragrant undertones make a sensory experience that whisks fans away to a wintry wonderland where every delectable mouthful encapsulates the season's freshness.

The recipe and baking technique of Peppermint Meltaways are meticulously crafted to provide their distinctive texture. Butter and cornstarch combine to create a soft and crumbly texture that virtually melts in your mouth. The lack of eggs in the recipe adds to the cookie's delicate texture, which makes it crumble easily and imparts a sense of sheer decadence. The careful blending of ingredients makes Peppermint Meltaways an exquisite confection that belies its simple ingredients.

When making peppermint meltaways, the dough is frequently rolled into bite-sized balls and baked until barely set. The cookies have a faint golden color as they come out of the oven, and the softness of their interiors balances their crumbly tops. The cookies morph after they're cooled and immerse themselves in a powdered sugar bath. This coating adds to the visual attractiveness of the cookies, making them look like a dusting of new snow, and also helps them melt in your mouth. The powdered sugar adds a subtle sweetness that melds well with the peppermint to create a harmonious blend of flavors and textures.

Because of their delicate texture and refreshing flavor, peppermint meltaways complement cookie platters and festive celebrations. They find their place in the tapestry of seasonal traditions. During the holidays, these cookies frequently take center stage in the culinary world, bringing back fond memories of previous winters and establishing new customs for future generations. Baking and sharing Peppermint Meltaways becomes a celebration of the season's spirit, an enduring act of love and joy spanning generations.

Beyond following the original recipe, inventive bakers have been experimenting with different approaches to bring their unique spin to this beloved holiday treat. Some recipes call for chocolate as a drizzle over the finished cookies or chocolate chips baked right into the dough. Chocolate and peppermint combine to provide a powerful combination that appeals to people who enjoy the classic pairing of these popular flavors.

Crushed candy canes or peppermint candies in the dough offer visual interest and an additional layer of crunch and intense peppermint flavor. The crushed candy's bright red and white fragments enhance the cookie's Christmas appearance by creating a beautiful mosaic. These versions highlight Peppermint Meltaways' versatility, enabling bakers to customize the recipe to their tastes and add fun surprises to their baked goods.

Beyond their delicious flavor, peppermint meltaways are frequently presented in a way that incorporates them into the visually stunning Christmas décor. Peppermint Meltaways become culinary decorations that add to the festive atmosphere when they are put in adorable cookie jars, decorated with festive ribbons, or placed in artistic tins. They are a visual and sensory feast due to their snow-like covering, delicate peppermint scent, and being a joy for the taste buds.

I love Peppermint Meltaways and giving them as gifts over the holidays. Delicious and meaningful presents may be shared with these neatly wrapped cookies adorned with colorful ribbons. When Peppermint Meltaways are given to friends, family, or coworkers, it becomes a gesture of kindness that cuts over linguistic and cultural divides and spreads the cheer and coziness of the season.

Peppermint Meltaways have a solid cultural resonance since they make people feel nostalgic and excited for the holidays. These cookies stand for the warm customs of winter, the delight of baking during the holidays, and the moments spent with loved ones that forge enduring memories. Peppermint Meltaways capture this unique time of year's charm, coziness, and tastes. They are perfect for enjoying a cup of hot cocoa by the fireplace or passing around during festive events.

To sum up, Peppermint Meltaways are proof of the charm of baking over the holidays. Their soft texture, reviving peppermint taste, and snow-like look make them a beloved confection that perfectly captures the spirit of winter celebrations. Peppermint Meltaways are a sensory experience beyond the typical, whether they are tasted in a quiet time of contemplation, shared with loved ones, or part of a cookie exchange. Not only do these cookies have a subtle peppermint flavor, but they also leave a happy aftertaste that perfectly captures the essence of the Christmas season. It's a delightful and unforgettable experience.

CHAPTER III

Beyond the Basics

Stained Glass Cookies: Edible Decorations

Regarding holiday sweets, Stained Glass Cookies stand out as visually stunning and stimulating treats. These quirky sweets captivate the mind with their vivid hues and transparent windows, evoking little pieces of stained glass art. Stained Glass Cookies, made from a basic sugar cookie foundation and decorated with vibrant candies, go beyond conventional baking to become delectable ornaments for festivities and holiday tables. This essay examines the background, the creativity, and the taste appeal of stained glass cookies, which turn them from a delicious delicacy into an edible work of ornamental art.

The rich tapestry of holiday baking customs is where Stained Glass Cookies began. Combining colorful candies to make translucent biscuit windows became popular in the middle of the 20th century. However, its exact roots still need to be discovered. The typical sugar cookie was elevated to an edible work of art by the inventive use of hard candies, which were crushed and put thoughtfully in the middle of cookie cutouts. As a result, cookies gained a whimsical and magical quality reminiscent of stained glass's beauty.

A basic yet adaptable sugar cookie batter is the cornerstone of Stained Glass Cookies. The basis comprises flour, butter, sugar, and a tiny touch of vanilla. This combination results in a canvas that is both delicate and robust enough to fall apart at the first bite. The size of the windows must be sufficient to display the vivid colors of the candy centers. Thus, accuracy in the cuts is just as important as the flavor of the cookies in ensuring success.

A key component of Stained Glass Cookies is the selection of candies, which affects the finished product's color scheme and aesthetic impact. The "stained glass" components of the cookie cutouts are made from carefully chosen hard candies in various colors that have been crushed into tiny pieces. The heart of each biscuit contains a carefully positioned candy, which ensures a uniform color distribution and a captivating mosaic appearance. Popular options include Jolly Ranchers or transparent fruit-flavored candies, each adding a distinct color to the stained glass pattern.

The magic happens when the sugar cookie dough bakes and encases the crushed candies, fusing flavors and textures in a harmonious whole. The candies melt and liquefy as the cookies bake, enlarging a transparent pool of brilliant color inside the cutouts. The end effect is a gorgeous display that resembles stained glass, and the candies' light-catching properties add even more visual fascination. A culinary alchemy that enthralls bakers and anyone lucky enough to watch the process, the conversion of uncooked dough into polished cookies. Stained Glass Cookies are praised for their adaptability and aesthetic value. The only restrictions on design are your creativity and imaginative bakers, who frequently play around with different cookie forms, hues, and configurations to create one-of-a-kind, customized masterpieces. Stained Glass Cookies offer an enjoyable and delectable canvas for artistic expression, ranging from traditional holiday forms like stars, angels, and

Christmas trees to more unusual patterns. The cookies transform from a simple sweet treat into an edible ornament that livens up any celebration.

The taste of these delicious treats is just as artistic as their external aspect regarding Stained Glass Cookies. The contrast between the oozy, sugary core and the crunchy, buttery sugar cookie produces a palate-pleasing sensory symphony. From the sound of the cookies crunching as teeth sank into the outer layer to the explosion of flavor and texture as the candy-filled middle was enjoyed, the cookies offer a multisensory experience. Stained Glass Cookies become more than just candies due to the harmonious fusion of flavor, texture, and visual spectacle; they become an immersive culinary experience.

Around the world, stained glass cookies are a part of many holiday customs and festivities. These cookies are essential to the holiday celebrations, whether placed on the dessert table at parties, hung from a Christmas tree, or given as adorable culinary presents. Baking Stained Glass Cookies may become a fun and social gathering place where friends and family can get together to create edible artwork. Cut out shapes, arrange candies, and watch the cookies change in the oven—all these activities become enjoyable.

The presentation of Stained Glass Cookies can also be used as a decorative element. Adding edible glitter, frosting, or a coating of powdered sugar may seem even more appealing. When stacked in pretty tins, tucked inside vibrant cupcake liners, or suspended with ribbons, Stained Glass Cookies transform from delicious candies into gorgeous culinary decorations. They are a pleasant addition to the visual extravaganza of the season because of their vivid colors and detailed designs, which provide a whimsical touch to Christmas décor.

Like any culinary tradition, there have been inventive reimaginings and modifications of stained glass cookies. To balance the sweetness of the sweets, some bakers experiment with different dough recipes, adding tastes like ginger, citrus, or almond. Some go beyond the conventional hard candies and experiment using different fillings like chocolate chunks, dried fruits, or even crushed nuts. These modifications highlight Stained Glass Cookies' versatility, enabling a combination of tastes and textures that gives an ageless classic a modern touch.
Finally, Stained Glass Cookies are proof of the fascinating fusion of seasonal celebrations and culinary creativity. Their vivid hues, clear windows, and delicious blend of textures produce a delight that appeals to the senses of sight and taste. Beyond being aesthetically pleasing, Stained Glass Cookies represent the wonder of turning ordinary materials into delectable works of art, the delight of artistic expression, and the coziness of group baking. With every delicious bite, these cookies capture the season's spirit and give a pop of color to holiday meals and gatherings. They also become a symbol of the festive mood.

Linzer Cookies: Elegant and Jam-Filled

Linzer sweets symbolize the union of tasteful tastes and classic design in refined and decadent sweets. These delicate delicacies, named after the Austrian city of Linz, combine a rich, almond-based dough with a delectable coating of fruit jam, perfectly encapsulating the craftsmanship of European pastry. Linzer Cookies, with their distinctive windowpane pattern and powdered sugar sprinkling, symbolize luxury and are frequently connected to celebrations, high tea, and the pleasure of indulging in sophisticated sweetness. This essay examines the history, the meticulous craftsmanship, and the mouthwatering taste combination that have made Linzer Cookies a timeless representation of sophistication in the baked goods industry.

The Linzer Torte, an Austrian delicacy that has been around since the 17th century, is where the Linzer cookie started. Its cookie equivalent was inspired by the Linzer Torte, a crumbly, almond-flavored pie packed with black currant preserves. This classic was made more delicate and bite-sized by the transition from torte to cookie, but it still had its unique flavor character. The Linzer Cookie evolved into a sophisticated treat that delighted the senses with its elaborate lattice structure and jewel-toned jam filling.

The almond-based dough, which gives the Linzer Cookie its unique nuttiness and crumbly texture, is its fundamental component. A combination of butter, sugar, and flour is combined with ground almonds or almond flour to make a rich yet delicate dough. Not only do almonds enhance the flavor of the cookie, but they also give it a soft chewiness and nuanced depth that distinguishes it from other butter-based cookies. Spices like cinnamon and occasionally a smidgeon of lemon zest are added to the dough to bring out its depth and create a pleasing interplay of flavors.

The unique windowpane shape of Linzer Cookies highlights the filling within, giving them an exquisite appearance. Usually, two similar dough rounds are cut out, with the top round carefully sliced to have a smaller shape in the middle, forming a "window" that lets some of the colorful jam show through. Because this procedure requires such accuracy, the cookies become edible artwork. Bakers frequently experiment with various cutout shapes and patterns. In addition to adding to the visual appeal, the lattice-like shape hints at what's inside: the sweet and fruity jam that completes the Linzer experience.

A key component of Linzer Cookies is the jam selection, which enhances the finished product's taste and appearance. Red currant jam is traditionally used to observe the original Linzer Torte. But the recipe has changed, and bakers now use a more comprehensive range of fruit preserves, such as apricot and blackberry, in addition to raspberry and strawberry. The visual appeal is enhanced by the jewel tones of the jam, which contrast magnificently with the golden-brown biscuit. The richness of the almond dough and the sweet-tartness of the jam combine to create a harmonic balance that characterizes the Linzer Cookie experience.

A delicate sprinkling of powdered sugar completes the look of Linzer Cookies. This last flourish brings a bit of refinement and intensifies the visual contrast between the bright jam, the golden biscuit, and the coating of snow. The powdered sugar adds a festive touch, making Linzer Cookies especially popular during the holidays by simulating a gentle snowfall. Baking becomes an artistic process when sugar is expertly sprinkled to create the right impact, resulting in a visual symphony that takes the cookies to a new level of sophistication.

Due to its grace and adaptability, Linzer Cookies have spread beyond their Austrian roots to become a popular dessert worldwide. They are perfect for every festive occasion, from weddings and afternoon tea parties to holiday get-togethers, because of their sophisticated look and elaborate design. Linzer Cookies are the ideal complement to a cup of tea or coffee because of their elegant tastes and delicate size, which elevates a routine break into a delightful moment. Linzer Cookies are not merely a delicious delicacy; they also represent culinary skill and sophisticated taste because of their relationship with special events and the detailed artistry that goes into their manufacture.

The adaptation of Linzer Cookies to many cultural contexts and seasonal inspirations is another example of their flexibility. When baking cookies, bakers frequently utilize their imagination, experimenting with various nut flours, spices, and jam tastes to produce distinctive varieties. Some versions add pecans or hazelnuts, giving the dough made chiefly of almonds a new flavor. Some experiment with unusual jams, such as passion fruit or fig, giving the conventional flavor profile a contemporary spin. Because Linzer Cookies are so versatile, there are countless ways to customize and experiment with their flavors.

The fact that Linzer Cookies are associated with holiday customs and festivities shows how culturally significant they are. Baking Linzer Cookies has become a beloved family tradition passed down through the generations in many homes. The lattice design's exquisite artistry and the jam's deliberate selection honor the European pastry traditions' long legacy of skill. The cookies lend a sense of refinement and nostalgia to the festive meal, typically serving as the focal point of dessert tables throughout the holidays.

Linzer Cookies are at the center of the Christmas gift-giving process as well. Arranged on festive cookie platters, inside beautiful boxes, or enclosed in artistic tins, these confections become symbols of love and skill in the kitchen. Giving Linzer Cookies as a present accomplishes two goals: it shares a tasty treat and exudes care and sophistication. They are perfect for expressing love, thanks, and warm holiday greetings because of their rich flavor and eye-catching appearance.

Finally, Linzer Cookies prove to be a lovely fusion of taste, workmanship, and tradition. These sophisticated candies, which have Austrian roots and are now considered a gastronomic treasure worldwide, perfectly capture the craftsmanship of European pastry in every mouthful. With their almond-based dough, elaborate lattice pattern, and jewel-toned jam filling, Linzer Cookies are a marvel at the fusion of flavor and design. These cookies transform into culinary pieces of art that represent elegance, tradition, and the delight of enjoying life's small pleasures as they adorn holiday tables and special events.

Thumbprint Cookies: Personalized Treats

Within the large category of handmade cookies, Thumbprint Cookies stand out as tasty, unique delicacies that appeal to makers and those lucky enough to taste them. These delicious cookies have earned a spot as beloved classics in the baking industry because of their unique thumbprint indentation filled with a range of sweet treats. Thumbprint Cookies are more than just a straightforward treat; they're a blank canvas for culinary creativity and customization, with many flavor combinations and filling options. This essay delves into the history, adaptability, and genuine happiness that Thumbprint Cookies offer to both makers and receivers.

Thumbprint Cookies date back to the middle of the 20th century, yet it still needs to be determined exactly where they came from, much like many other beloved recipes. These cookies are elementary and versatile, which makes them quite appealing. Usually consisting of butter, sugar, flour, and a small amount of vanilla, the basic dough provides bakers a flexible base to build their creativity. The endearing thumbprint indentation in the middle of each cookie distinguishes Thumbprint Cookies; it not only offers visual appeal but also acts as a receptacle for various delicious fillings.

Making Thumbprint Cookies is an enjoyable and tactile procedure. Little amounts of the dough are formed into balls and put on a baking pan once prepared. The secret is in the baker's indentation in the middle of each dough ball, which they do with their thumb or another appropriate utensil. This little gesture turns the cookies from ordinary rounds into individualized, hospitable jars ready to hold various delicious fillings. Each cookie becomes a one-of-a-kind, handcrafted product as the Thumbprint represents the baker's touch.

Thumbprint Cookies are pretty versatile since so many filling alternatives are available, which lets bakers customize the cookies to suit their tastes and the occasion. Jams, curds, and fruit preserves are common fillings that provide a tart and sweet contrast to the rich buttery texture of the cookie. Popular options include strawberry, raspberry, and apricot jams, which provide traditional fruit tastes and vivid hues. To add a little extravagance, you might pour some chocolate ganache, caramel, or Nutella into the Thumbprint to create a gooey, delicious core that contrasts with the crumbly outside of the cookie.

Bakers are experimenting with a broader range of nuts, spices, and extracts than just the classic options to give the dough and fillings depth. Cherry preserves, and almond extract-infused dough combines to create a mouthwatering almond-cherry symphony with every bite. Thumbprint Cookies are zesty and refreshing due to the combination of lemon curd filling and a dash of citrus zest in the dough. Thumbprint Cookies are a flexible and fascinating canvas for taste experimentation because of the recipe's versatility, which encourages culinary discovery.

As a result, thumbprint cookies are now inextricably linked to joyful occasions and holiday customs. They're perfect for parties and cookie exchanges because of their colorful design and personalized feel. Making thumbprint cookies is a beloved family tradition that brings generations together to roll, imprint, and fill these tiny jewels. The hues and tastes give cookie platters a celebratory feel, turning them from a sweet treat into a visual feast that celebrates happiness and community.

Giving Thumbprint Cookies as a present is more than just trading candies; it shows affection and consideration. Whether packaged in tasteful tins, adorned with colorful ribbons, or tucked into sophisticated boxes, these customized cookies create thoughtful and kind gifts. The time and care used to make each handprint and choose the ideal filling speaks to a sincere wish to spread happiness and pleasure. Thumbprint Cookies become delicious representations of love and happiness whether they are given as a hostess gift, a thank-you note, or a part of holiday celebrations.

Thumbprint Cookies' cultural resonance is seen by how well they adapt to different events and festivals throughout the globe. "Hallongrotta" or "Raspberry caves" are thumbprint cookies famous around Christmas and other special occasions in Scandinavian cultures. Similar cookies known as "Spitzbuben" are a favorite in Germany and are frequently filled with raspberry or apricot jam. These versions capture the universal appeal of thumbprint cookies, which transcend ethnic and culinary barriers with their simple delight of a buttery foundation and sweet filling.

The physical and artistic aspects of creating Thumbprint Cookies are just as appealing as their taste and look. These goodies become something special by hand-forming each cookie, imprinting it with a favorite food, and adding a personal touch. Each batch of Thumbprint Cookies is a unique and sentimental creation since the Thumbprint becomes a signature, a testament to the baker's originality and attention to detail.

Additionally, thumbprint cookies are a year-round favorite adaptable to seasonal variations due to their versatility. To invoke the season's flavors, they can be filled in the spring with colorful fruit compotes or citrus curds. During the summer, one may enjoy the taste of sunlight with every meal by utilizing fresh berries and tropical preserves. You may make a warm and soothing treat by nestling apple butter or pumpkin butter inside the thumbprints throughout the fall. A hint of seasonal enchantment can be added in the winter with the traditional pairing of rich chocolate ganache or fillings laced with peppermint.

The pleasure of Thumbprint Cookies comes from the collaborative process of creating and indulging in these customized delicacies rather than just eating them. The recipe for Thumbprint Cookies becomes a treasured family tradition, whether handed down through the years or found in a loved cookbook. Each cookie bears the warmth and affection of the hands who formed it, and the Thumbprint symbolizes that connection. As the cookies are eaten and shared, they serve as a means of making and keeping beautiful memories and being a lovely treat.

Finally, Thumbprint Cookies are proof of the delight that comes from crafting customized treats. From their modest beginnings to their reputation as a cherished classic, these cookies epitomize the coziness, originality, and handmade touch that characterize baked goods. Once just an indentation, the Thumbprint transforms into a symbol of uniqueness and attention to detail, making every cookie a one-of-a-kind creation. Thumbprint Cookies become more than simply candies as they adorn Christmas tables, gift boxes, and get-togethers; they transform into palatable representations of joy, love, and the basic pleasures of giving something thoughtful and handcrafted.

CHAPTER IV

Gluten-Free and Vegan Options

Almond Flour Sugar Cookies: Gluten-Free Bliss

Within the constantly changing world of baking, the world of gluten-free confections has seen a revolution, and leading this trend is the Almond Flour Sugar Cookie—a subtle and delicious substitute that dispels the myth that going gluten-free equates to sacrificing flavor. This delightful cookie, made with the benefits of finely ground almond flour, pleases even the pickiest eaters and accommodates those on restricted diets. Almond Flour Sugar Cookies are a mainstay in the diets of those looking for both pleasure and a wheat-free treat because of their mouthwatering taste and texture that belies their gluten-free status. This essay delves into the history, distinctive features, and culinary adaptability of Almond Flour Sugar Cookies, which serve as a monument to the skill of baking without gluten.

The growing need for gluten-free options without sacrificing flavor or texture is where Almond Flour Sugar Cookies originated. A prominent figure in this culinary revolution is almond flour, produced from finely ground almonds. Almond flour not only helps those with dietary limitations who must avoid gluten but also gives sugar cookies a unique nutty flavor and soft texture that take them to new heights. Consequently, each bite of the delicate, crumbly, somewhat chewy cookie entices the senses.

The main component of Almond Flour Sugar Cookies is almond flour. Almond flour offers a unique combination of benefits above all-purpose flour, used to create the framework of classic sugar cookies. Almond flour, which is high in protein, good fats, and a hint of sweetness, adds a nutty taste to the cookies, balancing their sweetness. Almond flour's finely ground texture adds to the delicate crumb of the cookie, making it melt-in-your-mouth delicious and defying the stereotype that gluten-free baked products are thick or dry by nature.

Almond flour sugar cookies are made similarly to regular sugar cookies but with a few modifications to account for the gluten-free aspect of the recipe. The key ingredients—butter, sugar, and vanilla—combine to create a tasty and creamy base. The gluten-free substitute is almond flour, which makes the dough a little more delicate yet incredibly malleable. The end product is a dough that comes together quickly, which is perfect for shaping, rolling, and cutting into the traditional shapes of sugar cookies, which bring back fond memories of baking. Almond Flour Sugar Cookies are incredibly versatile; inventive bakers have been known to experiment with different taste combinations and alterations of the basic recipe. A symphony of almond tastes in every mouthful may be achieved in certain dishes by adding a small amount of almond extract to bring out the nutty undertones. To improve the flavor profile, some people experiment with add-ins like chopped nuts, citrus zest, or even a tiny bit of spice. Almond flour's versatility allows bakers to add unique ideas and tastes to the cookie, transforming an ordinary recipe into a customized treat.

Even after baking, the delicate and fragile texture of these almond flour sugar cookies is one of their distinguishing features. Gluten is frequently used in traditional sugar cookies to give them structure and stop them from spreading too much as they bake. Because almond flour naturally has no gluten, these cookies can spread further, giving them a thin and deliciously chewy middle. The softly crispy edges provide a textural contrast that enhances the whole eating experience. Almond Flour Sugar Cookies differ from their conventional counterparts because this unique blend of textures adds to their blissful gluten-free status.

Although noticeable, the almond taste is not overbearing, which makes Almond Flour Sugar Cookies a tasty option for a wide range of people. For those watching their sugar consumption, the inherent sweetness of almond flour makes it possible to reduce the quantity of additional sugar in the recipe without sacrificing sweetness. The end product is a cookie that strikes the ideal balance between sweetness and subtlety, making it suitable for any time of day.

Almond Flour Sugar Cookies' culinary appeal goes beyond their inherent characteristics to include their ability to satisfy dietary requirements. People who have celiac disease or gluten sensitivity frequently find themselves shut out of the delights of traditional sugar cookies. Almond Flour Sugar Cookies provide a tasty and accommodating alternative free of gluten without compromising taste or texture. These cookies indicate that one's appreciation of delicious delicacies need not be restricted by dietary requirements.
Almond Flour Sugar Cookies are just as visually appealing as their conventional cousins. These cookies are perfect for various situations because of their rustic elegance, delicate crumb, and golden-brown color. Almond Flour Sugar Cookies hold a classic appeal when rolled, cut into festive forms, or dusted with powdered sugar, lending a

refined touch to cookie platters, dessert tables, and festivities. These cookies also provide a great blank canvas for frosting and decorating, allowing for creativity and customization thanks to the delicate almond flour crumb.

Around the holidays, when gift-giving, get-togethers, and cookie exchanges are significant, almond flour sugar cookies have grown in popularity. Being gluten-free makes them a thoughtful option for hosts who want to satisfy a range of dietary requirements from their visitors. When these cookies are presented in pretty boxes, garlanded with festive ribbons, or put in adorable tins, they become a tasty snack and a meaningful present that demonstrates consideration and inclusion.

Almond Flour Sugar Cookies have led the way in the realm of gluten-free baking when it comes to reinventing traditional recipes. They are unique among gluten-free snacks because of their soft crumb, nutty taste, and welcoming texture. Almond Flour Sugar Cookies smash the stereotype that flavor is limited by diet as they become increasingly well-liked and a staple on the tables of those looking for a delicious and gluten-free treat. With the help of these delicious cookies, the world of gluten-free baking opens up to a world of pleasant possibilities, demonstrating that a flavorful, gluten-free cookie can bring happiness to everyone.

Vegan Gingerbread Stars: Cruelty-Free Festivity

Vegan Gingerbread Stars is a beautiful example of a cruelty-free celebration that can be made during the holiday baking season. They prove that ethical choices don't have to be sacrificed for enjoyment. These plant-based delicacies, which have their roots in the rich history of gingerbread, encapsulate the spirit of seasonal warmth, spice, and delight while adhering to the values of sustainability and compassion. Making Vegan Gingerbread Stars is a deliberate reworking of the traditional recipe, substituting plant-based components for conventional ones without sacrificing flavor or history. This article examines the history, distinctive qualities, and cultural significance of Vegan Gingerbread Stars, which are not just a delicious treat but also a celebration of pleasure that is conscious and cruelty-free.

The history of European cooking is deeply ingrained in the centuries-old gingerbread tradition. Originally a sign of religious and cultural festivals, gingerbread has become a popular confection connected to celebrations, particularly in winter. Traditional components for classic gingerbread include butter, eggs, and molasses, which provide the recipe's rich flavor and delicate texture. However, Vegan Gingerbread Stars put a humane spin on a time-honored treat by reimagining this classic using plant-based components instead of traditional animal-based ones.

The thoughtful selection of plant-based components is the basis of Vegan Gingerbread Stars. Plant-based margarine or oils like coconut or vegetable oil can replace butter to supply the fat needed for a soft crumb. Eggs are frequently substituted with applesauce or mashed bananas, which give the dough moisture and binding qualities. An essential component of classic gingerbread, molasses continues to play a significant role in providing the cookies with their distinct dark color and rich, robust flavor. The distinctive warmth and scent that characterize gingerbread are imparted into the dough by the fragrant spices, which remain unaltered and include cinnamon, ginger, cloves, and nutmeg.

Vegan Gingerbread Stars are made similarly to their conventional counterparts. After mixing the wet and dry components, the dough is refrigerated to make handling and rolling easier. The kitchen is transformed into a festive workshop as the dough is rolled out and cut into positive star patterns, evoking a sense of tradition and expectation. The essence of gingerbread—a harmonic fusion of spice, sweetness, and warmth—permeates the atmosphere as the stars form, bringing in the spirit of the season.

The option to adopt a vegan gingerbread recipe goes beyond dietary restrictions. Many people who embrace a vegan lifestyle do so because they want to lessen the ecological impact that traditional animal agriculture has on the environment since they are committed to compassion and environmental sustainability. This idea is embodied by Vegan Gingerbread Stars, which provides a cruelty-free option that honors the lives and well-being of animals while embracing the holiday spirit.

The secret to making Vegan Gingerbread Stars is to blend flavors and textures just right without using components that come from animals. Because of its creamy richness, plant-based margarine works perfectly instead of butter to keep the cookies' soft, crumbly texture accurate to the traditional gingerbread recipe. Because applesauce or mashed bananas have binding qualities, they make up for the lack of eggs by keeping the dough together and adding a touch of sweetness. The warm, fragrant characteristics of the spices continue to be the essence of gingerbread, giving the cookies their classic Christmas vibe.

The kitchen turns into a sensory paradise as these vegan gingerbread stars bake. A plume of distinct aromas, including ginger, cinnamon, and molasses, fills the air and brings back fond memories of the holidays. The cookies are transformed from raw dough into golden-brown stars, each promising an enjoyment devoid of cruelty that welcomes others who are not vegan to enjoy the wonder of the holidays.

Beyond specific dietary preferences, Vegan Gingerbread Stars have a greater cultural significance as a symbol of inclusiveness. Plant-based diets are becoming increasingly popular, and these cookies represent celebrations with a wide range of tastes. Presenting Vegan Gingerbread Stars on a holiday table or at festive get-togethers, they give a tasty dessert that respects ethical principles while bridging dietary choices. These cookies help to create a celebration that is more empathetic and inclusive in this way.

Vegan Gingerbread Stars look festive when sprinkled with powdered sugar or drizzled with vegan icing, making them look even better. These cookies are made even more meaningful by adding the well-known star form, a timeless representation of enchantment and joy. Vegan Gingerbread Stars transform from a pleasure into culinary decorations that accentuate the warmth and charm of Christmas settings, whether arranged on festive plates, tucked into colorful tins, or strung as edible ornaments. Sharing these stars turns into a kind and compassionate deed that invites others to enjoy the happiness of a cruelty-free celebration.

Plant-based lifestyles' sustainability guiding principles align with Vegan Gingerbread Stars. These cookies are a responsible option for individuals who are worried about the environmental effects of their food choices because they don't include any components derived from animals, which helps to lessen the environmental impact of traditional animal agriculture. A tasty and environmentally friendly way to celebrate the holidays is with Vegan Gingerbread Stars, especially in light of global climate change and resource depletion struggles.

During the winter holidays, when gingerbread has a special place in many people's hearts, vegan gingerbread stars have grown in popularity. These stars provide a feeling of coziness and community whether consumed as a treat by the fireside, shared at special occasions, or given as a kind present. Beyond dietary restrictions, the sweets become a communal experience that invites everyone to partake in the delight of cruelty-free gingerbread and get into the holiday spirit.

To sum up, Vegan Gingerbread Stars is a tasteful combination of custom, kindness, and culinary innovation. Their sparkling forms, dancing on festive tables, reflect the season's romance, beckoning everyone to enjoy the pleasure of cruelty-free celebration. In addition to being tasty, these cookies represent a celebration of sustainability, diversity, and the common ideals that bring people together over the Christmas season. Vegan Gingerbread Stars are a delectable reminder that holiday indulgence can be joyful and morally grounded—a holiday that shows kindness to all living things and the earth we live on.

Tips for Adapting Recipes to Special Dietary Needs

The ability to modify recipes to meet specific dietary requirements is a vital talent that enables people to have a rich and varied gastronomic experience in the vast terrain of culinary tastes and dietary restrictions. Particular dietary demands cover various requirements, such as being gluten-free, vegan, and dairy-free. Ethical decisions, health concerns, or personal preferences can bring them on. By modifying recipes to accommodate these demands, people may enjoy well-known flavors
while following their specific dietary guidelines, opening

up a world of gastronomic possibilities. This essay examines helpful hints and factors to consider when adjusting recipes so that the joy of cooking and eating is inclusive and meets various requirements.

Understanding the fundamental concepts and components of the selected dietary limitations is the first step in customizing recipes to meet specific nutritional requirements. For example, anyone looking into gluten-free options should be aware of gluten-free flours and binding agents; similarly, people choosing a vegan diet should be mindful of plant-based dairy and egg substitutes. Learning about the particular dietary limitations lays the groundwork for well-informed ingredient replacements and adjustments.

Finding appropriate product substitutes that satisfy dietary restrictions is crucial to recipe adaptation. For instance, when baking without gluten, you can use rice flour, almond flour, or a gluten-free flour mix instead of wheat flour. Similarly, plant-based milk, coconut oil, or vegan butter can be substituted for dairy alternatives when choosing dairy-free products. Experimenting with various substitutes, tastes, and textures that satisfy specific dietary requirements may be found without sacrificing flavor.

It carefully considers the harmony of flavors and textures to modify recipes successfully. Ensuring the altered dish maintains the desired texture and taste character is crucial. In vegan cuisine, for example, where flaxseed or chia seed gel is frequently used instead of eggs, maintaining the proper amount of moisture and binding in the finished dish can be difficult. To create a harmonic mix, balancing tastes requires grasping the distinctive qualities of alternative components and modifying proportions accordingly.

It takes research and experimentation to modify recipes. It's best to approach recipe adjustments with an open mind and be ready to experiment with alternative component combinations. Before creating a whole meal, small-scale testing can be conducted to make necessary alterations and revisions so that the finished product satisfies taste and dietary compliance expectations. Maintaining a log of effective modifications adds to an expanding collection of go-to recipes customized for specific purposes.

A more thorough comprehension of food chemistry improves one's capacity for effective recipe adaptation. For instance, you may simulate the leavening qualities of eggs in vegan baking by mixing vinegar and baking soda or using plant-based yogurt. Even when following particular dietary restrictions, creating delicious and well-balanced foods is made more accessible by understanding the interactions between different components.

Naturally, many ethnic cuisines include foods that meet different dietary requirements. Investigating plant-based or gluten-free cuisines, such as Indian, Middle Eastern, or Asian cuisines, can inspire you and offer a variety of dishes that need little to no modification. These cuisines are an excellent resource for anyone looking to add variation to their modified recipes since they frequently use products and cooking methods that naturally accommodate particular dietary preferences.

Access to specialty foods catered to specific dietary requirements has increased. Products like dairy-free cheeses, plant-based protein substitutes, and gluten-free flours are made to make modifying recipes easier. It might be simpler to attain the intended outcomes by adding these specialist ingredients, which can improve the modified foods' taste profile and nutritional content.

Interacting with a helpful community facilitates navigating the realm of recipe modification. There are opportunities to exchange experiences, ask questions, and find tried-and-true modifications from others encountering similar dietary issues through online forums, social media groups, and local meet-ups. Gaining knowledge from the combined experience of a group of people creates a sense of community and motivates further experimentation in the kitchen.

Customizing taste profiles to meet specific dietary requirements is made possible by adapting recipes. For example, those on a low-sodium diet can experiment with citrus, herbs, and spices to add flavor without using too much salt. Tailoring flavor profiles guarantees that modified recipes match individual tastes and particular nutritional needs, resulting in a distinctly fulfilling meal experience.

It's critical to ensure that modified recipes preserve nutritional balance and deliver all the necessary elements without any deficits. For example, those switching to a plant-based diet should be mindful of their protein, calcium, iron, and vitamin B12 sources. Maintaining a healthy and well-rounded diet while meeting particular dietary demands can be accomplished by speaking with a nutritionist or researching plant-based sources of vital nutrients.

A greater awareness of cross-contamination is necessary when modifying recipes for those with dietary allergies or sensitivities. It's crucial to use distinct cutting boards, cooking surfaces, and kitchen tools for gluten-free modifications to avoid coming into touch with gluten-containing items. Keeping a specific area free of allergens for food preparation reduces the possibility of accidental exposure.

Flexibility is crucial when modifying recipes since it fosters inventive improvisation depending on component availability and individual tastes. Embracing flexibility means letting go of inhibitions, modifying recipes to fit the situation, and modifying amounts according to taste. Adaptability guarantees that the procedure is pleasurable and encourages a feeling of culinary inventiveness.

Creating recipe modifications for specific dietary requirements is a dynamic and empowering process. It takes experience, trial and error, and an openness to novel components and methods. Whether motivated by ethical, health, or personal preferences, the flexibility to alter recipes guarantees that people may enjoy a wide variety of delectable foods that meet their dietary needs. Modifying recipes becomes vital as the culinary scene develops, enabling everyone to enjoy preparing and sharing meals regardless of dietary restrictions.

CHAPTER V

Cookie Decorating Techniques

Royal Icing Basics: From Flood to Flow

When decorating cookies and cakes, Royal Icing is a flexible and indispensable tool that turns baked goods into delectable masterpieces. Because of its glossy texture, smooth consistency, and capacity to solidify into a surface resembling porcelain, Royal Icing has become a popular option for fine details, complicated designs, and breathtaking decorations. This essay explores the fundamentals of royal icing, including how it's made, how it might be used, and how to master the elusive balance between flow and flood, which is crucial for the success of icing-based embellishments on sweets.

Fundamentally, Royal Icing is just a straightforward concoction of water, meringue powder, and confectioners' sugar. This frosting is magical because it can change from having a thick, pipeable consistency to a silky, flowing one. The three main components each have a specific function: meringue powder adds solidity, confectioners' sugar gives structure, and water acts as a medium to get the right consistency. Finding the ideal proportions and perfecting the procedures that enable decorators to move between the flood and flow stages are necessary to achieve flawless Royal Icing.

The process starts with developing a thick, stable consistency that is sometimes called "piping consistency." This phase is essential for defining the structural components of a design, producing fine details, and defining forms. To get the perfect piping consistency, combine the confectioners' sugar and meringue powder mixture continuously while adding water gradually. The aim is to make a thick, smooth paste that maintains its shape when piped through a decorative tip. If the icing is too thin, it will become too soft to pipe fine features; if it is too thick, it will become challenging to see through.

The "flooding consistency" move comes next when the outlines and structural components are established. A little thinner icing that is still thick enough to hold its shape but still fluid enough to spread and fill in regions inside the outlines is what defines a flood consistency. It takes meticulous work to get the ideal flood consistency, incorporating water into the icing and stirring until the appropriate texture is reached. This step is essential for filling in the spaces between outlines to create a level and smooth surface for decorating.

The expertise and knowledge of a decorator are crucial in the art of creating flood uniformity. It calls for deeply comprehending the connection between the icing's thickness, flow, and settling properties. If the icing is too thin, it can spill over the outlines; if it is too thick, it might not spread evenly, creating an uneven surface. Finding an icing that is fluid enough to fill in gaps without losing control is the delicate balance; this thin line divides success from frustration.

Apart from the basic steps of piping and flooding uniformity, Royal Icing presents the exciting prospect of attaining a condition called "flow." Because flow consistency is even thinner than flood consistency, designers may create surfaces on cakes and biscuits that are seamless and flawless. To achieve flow, the icing must be made waterier until it is consistent with pouring cream.

When applied to cookies or cakes, this thin condition lets the icing settle into a perfect, glass-like sheen.

Learning the flow of Royal Icing is a sophisticated art that calls for accuracy, perseverance, and a thorough comprehension of the intended result. Decorators frequently utilize flow consistency to achieve a perfect surface for more elaborate patterns, cover extensive areas with a smooth finish, or create intricate backdrops. The trick is to control the icing's thinness to protect the surface uniformly without accidentally spreading or leaking.

Royal Icing is a preferred option for both professional and amateur cake decorators due to its many and varied uses. Mainly, cookies make a beautiful canvas for elaborate Royal Icing decorations. With Royal Icing, countless creative and personalized options are available, ranging from traditional sugar cookies with delicate floral decorations to elaborately piped holiday-themed delicacies. Royal Icing produces a smooth surface that is perfect for intricate patterns, and because it dries to a strong finish, decorations stay colorful and intact.
Royal Icing has a role in cake decoration, not just biscuits. Royal Icing is frequently used to make intricate decorations on cakes for weddings, birthdays, and other special occasions. Because of the medium's flexibility, designers may create anything they want, such as complex figures, personalized inscriptions, or delicate flowers and gorgeous lace patterns. The flawless texture that Royal Icing makes offers an ideal canvas for artistic expression, transforming cakes into both stunning and palatable works of art.
Beyond decoration, royal icing is also used in sugar art as an edible glue. The sturdy and long-lasting royal icing

adhesive holds cakes together with three-dimensional structures. Because of its adhesive properties, Royal Icing is a great tool for creating intricate cake toppers, tiered cakes, and edible sculptures.

When using Royal Icing, drying is essential, and decorators frequently use various methods to get the desired effects. When the icing is exposed to air, it dries and solidifies, forming a surface that maintains its shape. Decorators may use fans or dehumidifiers to improve air circulation and speed up drying. Furthermore, some decorators use the "wet-on-wet" method, which involves applying various icing colors while the foundation layer is still wet. This allows the colors to flow together perfectly and produce elaborate designs.

An additional creative expression layer is provided by coloring Royal Icing. Because they are concentrated and require less liquid to tint, gel-based food colors are a popular choice for Royal Icing. Achieving vivid and uniform color adds depth and individuality to the entire design, enhancing the visual impact of Royal Icing decorations.

While there are a lot of opportunities with Royal Icing, there are drawbacks as well. Humidity is one of the things that decorators have to deal with since it can change the icing's consistency and drying time. The learning curve is recognizing the subtleties of using Royal Icing in various environmental settings and modifying it as necessary. Additionally, decorators may first need help to achieve the proper uniformity and control since learning the skill of flooding and piping takes practice.

In addition to becoming a mainstay in the baking and cake decorating industries, royal icing has become a much-loved holiday custom. Using Royal Icing to decorate cookies for the holidays has become a beloved custom among family and friends. Cookie decorating parties, where people get together to decorate their cookies with vibrant Royal Icing, have developed into a fun and artistic custom that promotes a sense of community and celebration.

In summary, Royal Icing is a fundamental ingredient in edible art, providing decorators with the tools to turn baked goods into aesthetically spectacular and delectable works of art. Decorating cakes and cookies becomes more sophisticated as one moves from piping to flooding, striking the perfect balance between uniformity and flow. Decorators embark on a creative journey that blends technical proficiency with artistic expression as they investigate the possibilities of Royal Icing, transforming typical candies into delectable works of beauty that satiate the senses and brighten any occasion.

Piping and Flooding: Creating Intricate Designs

The combination of piping and flooding methods is vital in confectionery art that turns baked products from everyday delights into delectable works of beauty. These two powerful tools—frequently used in conjunction with Royal Icing—allow decorators to create elaborate patterns, customized decorations, and intricate motifs on cakes, cookies, and other baked goods. Flooding adds a thinner consistency to fill areas and produce a smooth, continuous surface, whereas piping is the meticulous application of thick icing to delineate structural parts and create contours. This article explores the strategies, difficulties, and creative possibilities of combining flooding and piping. It also dives into the art and nuances of these two processes.

Piping provides the structure and definition that form the basis for complex designs, enabling the creation of an adorned masterpiece. The first step in the procedure is to prepare a piping consistency that is thick enough to maintain its form when piped through a decorative tip, which is called royal icing. Decorators frequently utilize a variety of tips, including petal tips for producing floral components, star tips for ornamental borders, and round tips for drawing thin lines. The tip selection and the icing consistency are critical elements affecting how the design turns out.

Decorators can define forms, create complex patterns, and define the outlines of a design with precision thanks to piping. Decorators have a level of control over the thickness of the lines that is essential for creating crisp, well-defined contours because of the pressure given to the piping bag. Decorators run the piping tip over the baked good's surface, allowing the icing to run out and harden as it comes into touch with air. The decorator's idea becomes concrete lines and shapes through this transforming process, creating the finished masterpiece's blueprint.

The piping skill goes beyond simple outline work; decorators frequently employ it to produce three-dimensional components, complex lace designs, and custom text. Decorators may give their patterns depth and dimension by manipulating the icing's flow. For instance, a deft touch and an acute eye for uniformity and spacing are needed to create the delicate petals of a flower or the complex loops of lace. The ability of the decorator to transfer inventiveness into accurate and aesthetically pleasing details is the key to mastering piping.

Flooding adds a contrasting approach that creates smoothness and continuity to the design, while piping gives the framework. Flood regularity Because royal icing is thinner than piping, it may fill in the gaps and flow more readily inside the shapes that the piping step made. It takes careful mixing and adding water to the icing to get the correct flood consistency and texture. This step is essential for producing a smooth surface and serving as a blank canvas for additional ornamentation.

Similar to painting inside the lines, flooding is accomplished by decorators using the flow of Royal Icing rather than a brush to create a smooth, level surface. The tricky part is striking the right balance between control and thinness. If the icing is too thick, it may not spread uniformly and create an uneven surface; if it is too thin, it may spill over the outlines. A steady touch and a systematic approach are necessary for successful flooding to maintain the design's clarity and definition.

Floods and piping work together like a beautiful dance that starts with the basic shapes and grows from there. The "dam and fill" technique is a common term decorators use to describe pipetting thicker icing around a design's edges to form a barrier or "dam." This barrier allows the flood-consistency ice to settle and fill the allocated space evenly, preventing it from pouring over the edges. Consequently, the smoothness of flooding and the accuracy of piping are combined in a seamless design. The

combination of floods and pipes creates a world of imaginative possibilities. Decorators may utilize this combination to create individualized designs, ornate backdrops, and detailed scenarios that perfectly encapsulate a theme or event. To produce the intended visual impression, decorators typically take a strategic approach, outlining the sequence in which specific pieces will be piped and flooded. The end product is a unified and stunning design that showcases the decorator's talent and creative vision.

Although floods and piping provide many creative possibilities, they pose particular difficulties for designers. It takes skill, persistence, and a thorough grasp of the medium to get the proper consistency for flooding and piping. The narrow line between thickness that preserves structure and thinness that permits a seamless flow is one that decorators frequently have to walk. Trial and error is a part of the learning curve, and decorators modify their methods and formulas according to the results of each try.

The success of floods and piping is also significantly influenced by environmental conditions. The ability of the decorator to transition smoothly between the piping and flooding stages can be impacted by humidity levels, which can also affect how long Royal Icing takes to dry. High humidity might cause Royal Icing to dry more slowly. Therefore, decorators should be patient and modify their workflow accordingly. On the other hand, in low-humidity settings, the ice can dry faster, requiring rapid thinking and prompt action.

Another level of intricacy is added by the selection of colors and how well they work with the material. Gel-based food coloring is necessary to get bright and uniform colors. Still, decorators must also consider the possibility of color mixing or bleed during the flooding phase. Decorators can manipulate color interactions and produce aesthetically pleasing patterns by employing techniques like applying neighboring colors after layers have dried or applying a "wet-on-wet" approach.

The skill of flooding and piping continues to enthrall designers and bakers alike despite the difficulties. Cookie decorating parties have gained popularity for showcasing creativity and friendship. Participants assemble to pipe and flood their masterpieces. Often, the elaborate patterns generated by flooding and piping become delicious representations of happiness, love, and the basic joys of giving something handcrafted and sincere.

In summary, the fundamental element of confectionery artistry is the dynamic interaction between flooding and piping, which turns baked items into edible canvases for artistic creations. Flooding adds a smooth and seamless finish, while piping gives the features and structure that characterize a design. Combining these two methods calls for skill, accuracy, and an artistic vision that goes beyond the bounds of the medium. When decorators become proficient in flooding and piping, they open a realm of creative expression that transforms commonplace foods into aesthetically magnificent and delicious works of art.

Edible Paints and Glazes: Unleashing Your Artistic Side

Edible paints and glazes are the canvas on which the union of art and baking is created in culinary innovation. With these adaptable media, bakers and decorators can go beyond conventional limitations and create customized works of art that are visually stunning as well as a culinary feast. Artists may unleash their creativity on cookies, cakes, and other confections with the palette of possibilities provided by edible paints and glazes. This essay explores the realm of edible paints and glazes,
looking at their composition, uses, and endless
possibilities at the nexus of baking and art.

Decorators may add vivid colors and detailed features to their works with edible paints, usually created with food-grade colorants and extracts. Because the paints are made with edible components, the creative decorations are entirely edible and pleasing. Edible paintings can be applied by artists using brushes, sponges, or even airbrushing techniques to the outside of cookies, cakes, or sweets coated in fondant. The art of baking is elevated by the ability to paint directly onto edible canvases, which enables decorators to express their creativity with precision and degree of detail previously only possible with traditional painting.

The success of edible paints is mainly dependent on their composition. Food-grade coloring agents come in various hues that may be combined to create the necessary tints. They are often in the form of gels or powdered pigments. Because these colorants are made especially for cooking, they adhere to safety regulations and maintain the taste and texture of baked goods. The liquid part of the paint is made up of extracts like lemon or clear vanilla extract, which provide flavor and give the paint the consistency needed to paint. Combining these ingredients creates a flexible and tasty painting medium that allows for new possibilities for artistic expression.

When decorators explore the world of glazes, an edible gloss that gives baked goods a sophisticated, lustrous shine and artistic freedom blossoms, decorators can improve the visual appeal of their delights by using glazes, which come in clear or colored tints. Edible glazes for decoration can include extra components like gelatin or corn syrup to provide a smooth and glossy surface. However, classic glazes can be made with powdered sugar and liquids like milk or juice. Glazes turn dull surfaces into brilliant canvases that serve as a glossy canvas for further creative embellishments.

Applying edible paints and glazes requires skill, discernment, and imagination. Decorators frequently start by using Royal Icing to outline their patterns using piping or flooding techniques, establishing the foundation for developing creative expression. Edible paints become helpful once the foundation is created, enabling decorators to add minute details, patterns, and lines. Artists can create a variety of textures and effects by using brushes of varied sizes as their preferred tools. The paints can be blended and layered, adding depth and dimension that improve the design's overall visual impact.

Edible paints may be used for more than just conventional painting methods. A prevalent technique in traditional art, airbrushing has made its way into the field of cake decorating and confectionery creation. Decorators apply gradients, shadows, and complex patterns to baked delicacies using airbrush equipment to spray edible paints onto their surfaces. A level of control and accuracy that is especially useful for producing smooth color transitions and aesthetically striking effects is provided by airbrushing. Edible paints may be airbrushed to lend a touch of creativity to baked items, such as shading fondant-covered cakes or creating ethereal backdrops on biscuits. This technique takes baked goods to new heights.

Edible paints and glazes appeal due to their flexibility and spontaneity throughout the creative process and striking visual effects. Decorators can try various brushstrokes, methods, and color combinations since they know that creative endeavors are acceptable and encouraged. Because edible paints are so flexible, designers may make necessary repairs and tweaks until the desired outcome is achieved. This adaptability encourages delight and creativity, transforming decorating into a culinary art therapy.

Mainly, cookies are excellent canvases for glazing and painting with food substances. The glossy exteriors of gingerbread or sugar biscuits make a beautiful background for elaborate patterns and vivid hues. From carefully glazed backgrounds to hand-painted watercolor effects, cookies are transformed into tasty works of art that inspire amazement and joy. Using edible paints and glazes to decorate cookies turns into a beloved holiday and special occasion ritual when friends and family celebrate the art of edible painting and let their imaginations run wild.

Cakes may be elevated beyond cookies to the status of works of art by using edible paints and glazes. Wedding cakes provide an artistic canvas, as cake designers use edible paints to create unique designs that capture the couple's style, color scheme, and theme. Glazes are applied to cakes coated in fondant to enhance their beauty and provide a glossy sheen that exudes refinement and appeal. Edible paints and glazes may be used to create intricate designs on cakes, such as exquisite watercolor patterns or hand-painted floral motifs, that fascinate the senses and the eyes.

Baking and art combine particularly well in the realm of fondant-covered confections. Cakes may be transformed into sculptures using fondant, which offers a smooth and pliable surface that is easy to work with for edible paints and glazes. Artists can paint elaborate scenarios, represent figures, or even imitate well-known art pieces on fondant-covered canvases. Edible glazes produce a glossy sheen that amplifies the visual impact and gives the piece a polished, businesslike appearance. Fondant-covered cakes transform into delicious sweets and interactive culinary art pieces that elicit strong feelings and convey a narrative.

Applying edible paints and glazes gives designers much creative freedom but also comes with specific difficulties. Easing the consistency of edible paints is a delicate mix between control and fluidity, especially when dealing with detailed drawings. Decorators must go through the learning curve brought on by various brushes, painting methods, and drying times. The difficulty is perfecting the mixing, layering, and adding the right intricacy without sacrificing the baked products' structural integrity.

The drying period of edible paints and glazes can be affected by environmental elements like humidity. Therefore, artists must modify their methods according to the current circumstances. Longer drying durations may be required in humid climates, whereas faster drying times and possible effects on color mixing may occur in drier environments. As decorators dive farther into the realm of edible painting and glazing, they acquire the expertise of adjusting the process to account for these factors.

Beyond the world of professional decorators, home bakers, and fans find a place in their hearts for the creativity of edible paints and glazes. The availability of edible paints and glazes has encouraged people to express their creativity and transform everyday baked items into works of art with a dash of personality. Cookie decorating parties have gained popularity as a way to enjoy the fun of making edible art together. Friends and family join together to paint and polish their goodies.

To summarize, edible paints and glazes have become popular as revolutionary materials connecting baking and art. Applying glossy finishes to confections and paint directly onto edible canvases offers designers creative freedom never seen before. Delicious paints and glazes turn baked foods into delicious works of art, whether applied to cookies to create intricate motifs, cakes coated in fondant to add shine, or cakes airbrushed with ethereal backdrops. When culinary skill and creative vision combine, it becomes a celebration of creativity that transforms typical delicacies into individualized, visually spectacular masterpieces that satisfy the tongue and the eyes.

CHAPTER VI

Gift-Giving and Packaging Ideas

Creating Cookie Gift Boxes: A Thoughtful Gesture

Few things in the pleasant world of gift-giving arouse as much warmth and happiness as delivering a well-chosen cookie gift box. A box of thoughtfully handcrafted cookies is more than just a tasty treat; it represents love, sharing, and the happiness of homemade deliciousness. Whether it's for holidays, special events, or to make someone smile, the skill of making cookie gift boxes elevates a straightforward culinary project into a sincere demonstration of thoughtfulness and imagination. This essay explores the qualities that make cookie gift boxes a beloved and kind gesture in gifting, delving into its appeal and importance.

Baking, a labor of love that goes beyond the kitchen and becomes a concrete manifestation of caring, is at the center of the cookie gift box. The first step in the process is picking the appropriate recipes and tastes based on the occasion or the recipient's preferences. The selection of sweet goodies is as varied as the personalities and palates of the people who will indulge in them, ranging from traditional chocolate chip cookies to festive gingerbread sweets. Because each cookie is imbued with intention and the desire to produce something unique for someone special, baking itself takes on significance.

A gift box's cookie selection enables a tasteful fusion of textures, tastes, and forms. A well-chosen collection might have various cookies, including chewy and soft types, crunchy treats, and cookies with chocolate drizzling or multicolored frosting. In addition to providing a sense of surprise, the variety of textures and flavors also accommodates a range of palates, guaranteeing that each receiver will find something enjoyable in the box. Whether the cookies are visually appealing due to elaborate patterns or colorful decorations, they add to the whole experience and make the gift box an eye- and palate-pleasing feast.

The present-giving experience is enhanced by the cookie gift box's design, which builds delicious anticipation even before the receiver bites into the treat. The presentation lends a sense of refinement and elegance, whether displayed in traditional cookie tins or adorable boxes with bows and ribbons. Custom labels or tags on packaging let the maker express a sentimental message or commemorate a special occasion. A basic box of cookies becomes a visual feast due to the presentational effort, representing the thought and care that go into a considerate gift.

The impact of a cookie gift box mostly depends on the time and occasion and its physical components. The occasion, be it a birthday, a holiday, or a thank-you present, strengthens the meaning behind the offering. Biscuits with a holiday motif are festive, while cozy biscuits may offer consolation in trying times. Giving cookies as a present allows people to connect, celebrate, and express their feelings, making a simple transaction unique and heartfelt.

Making cookie gift boxes turns into a culinary art. Cookies may be made into little works of art by adding personalized touches with decorative ingredients like fondant, frosting, or edible paints. You may customize themes to fit the occasion or the receiver's hobbies. For example, you might give a fan a selection of cookies with a sports theme or an assortment of flower arrangements for a spring celebration. The cookies are a blank canvas for artistic expression, and the time and care used to decorate them add even more sentimentality and affection.

The element of surprise is crucial in the world of cookie gift boxes. The recipient discovers a unique flavor or texture with every cookie, making every mouthful an experience. The thrill of not knowing what's inside the box adds to the excitement and makes the encounter unforgettable. A variety of cookies makes the present stand out and provides a pleasurable voyage through various tastes and sensations. Consider including a mix of traditional favorites and creative innovations.

You may also personalize cookie gift boxes according to dietary requirements or preferences. Making a gift box that accommodates a recipient's gluten-free, vegan, or other specific diet demonstrates a higher degree of concern in a society where people may follow these diets. Almond flour cookies free of gluten, vegan chocolate chip treats, or nut-free sugar cookies are inclusive choices that let everyone enjoy the happiness of a handcrafted treat. In addition to being tasty, the meticulous customization of the gift box guarantees that the gesture is flexible and sensitive to the recipient's demands.

Giving baked cookies as a present celebrates the cookies themselves and the love, labor, and time that went into making them. In a society where convenience frequently takes precedence over slowness, creating and giving cookies is a conscious decision to take time to slow down and participate in a meaningful process. This action emphasizes the importance of unique and homemade touches and supports the notion that the most meaningful gifts are those that hold a part of the giver's heart.

Cookie gift boxes are shared by more people than just the intended recipient; they become a social gathering point. It is designed to be shared and enjoyed with friends, family, and coworkers as you open a box of baked cookies. As people join together to enjoy the sweet treats, it triggers camaraderie and joyful moments. Sharing cookies creates a sense of belonging and improves relationships, making a plain treat box the starting point for special times spent with others and enduring memories.

In the era of digital connections, when loved ones may be separated by physical distance, sending or receiving cookie gift boxes is a concrete means of bridging the gap. A box of thoughtfully wrapped cookies may convey the spirit of connection, love, and home to someone far away. Despite the distance in kilometers between the donor and the recipient, thinking behind it creates a shared experience. It serves as a reminder that the comfort of handmade sweetness may go any distance, even without physical presence.

Cookie box makers and chefs are not the only people who can make and present cookie boxes. People of all skill levels are welcome to participate in this fun and approachable activity. As their confidence builds, novice bakers may progressively experiment with varied tastes and embellishments by starting with more straightforward recipes. Every batch of cookies symbolizes a new chapter in the baker's culinary journey, and learning and improvement become essential to the gift-giving experience.

To sum up, making cookie gift boxes is a kind and considerate gesture that extends beyond baking. Every cookie is infused with love, creativity, and time, transforming the baking process into a heartfelt way to show support. Cookie gift boxes are a pleasant and unforgettable way to celebrate occasions, connect with others, and spread the joy of handmade goodness. This is because of the well-chosen selection, unique presentation, and the caring behind the gesture. A box of handcrafted cookies is a tribute to the enduring worth of handmade, emotional gestures of love and generosity in a world when presents are frequently mass-produced and impersonal.

Packaging Tips for Freshness and Presentation

Food presentation is an art form in and of itself, particularly with handcrafted goodies like cookies. It's not only about the flavors and sensations. Proper wrapping greatly influences the freshness of the contents and the gift's aesthetic appeal. How you package your cookies may significantly affect the recipient's experience, whether selling them or sharing them with close friends and family. This essay looks at crucial packing advice to keep your delicious cookies fresh and show them in a way that appeals to the eye and guarantees they arrive at their destination undamaged.

Choosing the appropriate packing materials is the first step in keeping your cookies fresh. Because they provide a barrier against outside factors that might deteriorate the cookies' quality, airtight containers or resealable bags are the best options. Sealing packages tightly keeps out air, which can cause staleness and moisture loss. Once the item has been opened, the receiver may easily access the contents and preserve its freshness by resealing the bag, made possible by resealable bags with zipper closures.

When selecting packing materials, consider the type of cookies you sell. Individual wrapping may benefit delicate or decorated cookies to avoid breakage or harm to elaborate decorations. While protecting cookies from external elements and physical contact, cellophane or clear plastic wrap allows viewing. Stickier cookies, such as shortbread or biscotti, could work better in layers within an airtight tin or other sturdy container. Adapting your packaging strategy to the unique qualities of your cookies guarantees they reach their destination just as tasty and aesthetically pleasing as they did when they were taken out of your kitchen.

Incorporating layers into the container helps maintain freshness and makes for a visually pleasing display. Think of sandwiching wax paper or parchment between layers of cookies when assembling them. This step keeps cookies from adhering to one another, particularly when they have frosting, glaze, or other toppings. It also lessens the possibility of damage during transit and makes separation simple. Layering becomes very important in preserving the unique flavors and textures of each variety of cookies while packing them together, layering moisture-absorbing components in the packaging to counteract humidity and keep your cookies crisp. Particularly for cookies with delicate crusts or coatings, moisture can cause sogginess and impair the quality. You may protect the cookies from the dangers of humidity by adding silica gel packets or even a little sachet of raw rice to absorb excess moisture. This safety measure becomes particularly pertinent when shipping cookies to regions with different climates, highlighting the significance of customizing your packing to the destination's requirements.

Effectively sealing your package is essential to preserving freshness and guarding against outside factors eroding the quality of your cookies. Make sure the zipper is firmly closed to produce an airtight seal using resealable bags. Ensure containers with lids are securely fastened and locked to stop air from leaking. For an additional layer of protection, use shrink wrap or food-grade plastic wrap. Along with maintaining freshness, a tight seal gives your cookies' presentation a polished appearance.

Putting a personal touch on your packaging makes a great present and highlights the thought and work that went into making your homemade delights. Consider adding labels, tags, or handwritten remarks to accentuate the tastes or convey a message. A joyful and celebratory touch is added when themed packaging is used, particularly for holidays or other special events. A plain container may be transformed into a present that pleases the eyes and the palate with ribbons, twine, or bows.

When delivering cookies, the packaging needs to guarantee their freshness, look good, and offer sufficient protection against the rigors of transit. Choose shipping boxes that are robust enough to endure handling and any knocks while en route. The danger of breakage or damage can be decreased by enclosing the cookie containers in cushioning material, such as bubble wrap or packing peanuts. To notify carriers of the package's sensitive contents, clearly mark it as fragile and give handling recommendations.
Think of giving each cookie a unique presentation within the enormous container in addition to the outer wrapping. Create tiny assortments within the more significant gift if you've made a range of cookies so that recipients may

sample different flavors without opening the entire collection. Delightful surprise elements can be found in little, separate treat bags or chambers inside the packaging, so browsing the range is like opening a box of tasty delights.

Consider adding additional protection if some of your cookies' components are delicate or have detailed decorations. To avoid breakage and maintain the aesthetic integrity of the embellishments, wrap each cookie individually in transparent cellophane or place them inside little boxes. Because of this meticulous attention to detail, every cookie is presented with care and arrives in perfect shape.

The method and time of transportation are essential considerations when gift-giving cookies to ensure their freshness. If some of the components in the cookies have a shorter shelf life than others, choose expedited delivery to reduce the time they spend en route. To prevent shipment during periods of excessive heat that might affect the quality of the cookies, check the weather at the destination. Let the receiver know when you expect the box so they can be sure to get it on time and keep or refrigerate the cookies when they arrive.

Finding the ideal balance between protection and usefulness is crucial since the size and weight of your packing might affect shipping costs. Although the cookies must be adequately cushioned and protected, reducing unnecessary weight reduces transportation costs.

Consider the package's total size and look into affordable delivery choices that will maintain the contents' integrity. Adequate packaging makes sure that your kind gift is still within your means.

Finish off by attaching handling and storage guidelines to your cookie gift box. Advise on how to keep food fresh, including freezing, refrigerating, and airtight-keeping methods. To guarantee that the recipients can savor the delicacies at their finest, make sure you disclose any shelf-life information about the cookies. These instructions enable recipients to enjoy the cookies at their best and add a kind touch.

In summary, the skill of packing baked cookies requires a careful balancing act between maintaining freshness and presenting the delicacies in a visually appealing way. Use airtight jars, moisture-absorbing materials, and tight seals to keep your cookies fresh. An aesthetically pleasing appearance is enhanced by layering within the container, personalization, and focus on each cookie. Reliable packing, safety precautions, and effective delivery methods are essential when sending cookies. A basic box of cookies can become a joyful and enduring display of care and artistry with thoughtful packaging, protecting the quality of your baked goods and improving the whole presenting experience.

Homemade Tags and Labels: Adding a Personal Touch

Giving is more than just the delicious content regarding baked goods and culinary delights. Adding handmade tags and labels elevates the presentation of a thoughtful gift; it adds a personal touch that turns an ordinary contribution into a personalized and touching gesture. Handmade tags and labels provide a touch of personalization and skill to items like jars of jam, biscuit boxes, and bottles of infused oil. This article examines the significance of handmade tags and labels and how they may be used to personalize presents, improve their overall appearance, and leave a lasting impression on the receiver.

Making handmade tags and labels is fundamentally a celebration of uniqueness and ingenuity. It offers a chance to add some of the giver's individuality to the presentation, transforming an ordinary container into something unique. The first step in the process is to select the appropriate materials, whether it's cardstock, textured paper, or even recycled materials. This decision affects the recipient's physical experience when they hold the present and sets the tone for the entire design.

How the tags and labels are designed is the next step in customizing. The design captures the essence of the present, the topic, or the event, whether printed, hand-drawn, or a combination of the two. The tag for a batch of handmade cookies may have cutesy pictures of the several kinds of cookies within. In the same way, a label for a jar of handmade pickles may have colorful pictures of the veggies used or the pickled process itself. The design becomes a visual storyteller that provides an insight into the planning and work that went into making the handmade treat.

Personalization includes more than just aesthetics; it also includes sentimental quotes or words of gratitude. Warm, handwritten remarks or sentiments on the tags and labels evoke attentiveness and connection. Gift-giving becomes a significant emotional exchange when it includes words such as "Made with love" or a personalized note for the recipient. In a time where texting is frequently preferred over other forms of communication, the handwritten component of the present takes on sentimental value.

The information that homemade tags and labels provide regarding the contents of the gift is quite essential. Labels for jams, chutneys, and infused oils created at home can provide information on the ingredients used, specific storage or consumption guidelines, and even the creation date. This educational component gives the handmade work a polished appearance while improving the recipient's user experience. By providing such information, you show that you value openness and give the receiver peace of mind so they may enjoy their present.

The capacity of handmade tags and labels to be used for various gift-giving events demonstrates their versatility. Personalization is possible with tags and labels matching every event's theme and atmosphere, from holidays and birthdays to weddings and housewarmings. A jar of housemade honey with a label that has flowery and golden tones is a suitable present for a springtime event. On the other hand, a jar of spiced nuts with labels that remind you of fall hues adds coziness to a winter party. Thanks to this flexibility, the donor may construct a coherent and themed presentation that fits the occasion.

Handmade tags and labels become an essential element of the overall presentation of edible presents. With images or visuals that capture the spirit of the homemade item, the design can mirror the flavor profile of the ingredients. A jar of sugar infused with lavender may have tags with pretty lavender drawings, while a bottle of handmade vanilla extract might have images of vanilla beans. The visual attractiveness is enhanced by this theme of uniformity, giving the receiver a sneak peek at the sensual experience they might expect.

Not just graphic designers or talented craftspeople can make handcrafted tags and labels. People of all skill levels are welcome to engage in this approach, which is both approachable and entertaining. For individuals with less experience with graphic design, easily navigable solutions are available through templates, clip art, and online creative tools. Inexperienced crafters can make visually appealing tags and labels that match the gift's overall aesthetic by experimenting with typefaces, colors, and layouts. Creating handmade tags extends the creative process and gives donors a platform to express themselves while feeling good about adding a unique touch to presents.

Handmade tags and labels fit with the thoughtful gifting attitude in the age of conscious consumerism, when people appreciate the care and work that goes into a present. Making something by hand expresses a desire for authenticity and a break from generic, mass-produced goods. It conveys a dedication to the receiver that goes beyond the gift's tangible value—an expenditure of time and imagination that enhances the meaning behind the action. Handmade labels and tags represent a closer bond and a deliberate decision to share something thoughtfully prepared.

Adding handcrafted labels and tags makes the donor feel proud and in control. It turns giving gifts into a way for people to express themselves and shows their originality and attention to detail. The happiness one feels upon seeing a present that has been painstakingly decorated and tagged with a name stays long after the item is exchanged. It becomes a source of fulfillment and a concrete illustration of the work in making a thoughtful and unforgettable gift.

When branding handmade goods, homemade tags and labels are essential, particularly for individuals who own small or home-based enterprises. Maintaining design consistency across various items produces a recognized and coherent brand identity. Using tags and labels to create a consistent visual concept for handmade jams, baked products, or candles may increase brand identification. This branding component becomes especially important for small-scale artisanal ventures, internet platforms, or local markets where items stand out due to their unique identities.

Handmade tags and labels offer a chance to adopt eco-friendly behaviors in sustainability and ecologically aware living. Selecting recyclable or biodegradable materials is consistent with the philosophy of cutting waste and gift packaging's environmental effects. Crafters should investigate environmentally friendly printing solutions, such as soy-based inks, to further improve the sustainability of their handcrafted tags and labels. This awareness of the environment indicates a thoughtful gift-giving strategy that goes beyond the recipient's happiness to include a duty to the environment.

Handmade labels and tags effectively give gifts a personalized touch and transform the gifting process into a unique and meaningful exchange. These handcrafted components express attention, originality, and dedication to the receiver and their visual attractiveness. Handmade tags may be tailored to fit a variety of themes and situations, which makes gift-giving an even more enjoyable experience. A letter written by hand or a label with meticulous planning, the addition of handmade tags becomes a celebration of uniqueness and a monument to the ageless appeal of customized gestures in the art of giving.

CHAPTER VII

Cookie Exchange Parties

Hosting a Successful Cookie Swap

The cookie swap is a joyful celebration of culinary talent, fellowship, and the joy of exchanging handmade cookies, making it stand out in the festive tapestry of Christmas customs. Friends, family, and neighbors get together for this customary get-together, during which everybody contributes a batch of their best cookies to share and enjoy. The cookie swap is an event that offers more than simply indulging in delicious treats; it's a chance to demonstrate one's culinary skills, sample a variety of tastes, and make enduring memories. This essay explores the essential components that add to the charm of this cherished custom, delving into the art of organizing a successful cookie exchange.

A successful cookie swap is built on meticulous preparation and well-thought-out coordination. First, decide on a date far in advance, ensuring it falls within the holiday season and fits into the schedules of interested parties. Send out invites to neighbors, friends, and family as soon as the date is decided. Make sure the guest list includes both known individuals and possible newcomers. Consider the space and resources available when determining the number of attendees; try to strike a balance that will enable a wide variety of cookies while preserving a cozy and friendly ambiance.

Encourage attendees to select their cookie recipes in advance to create a sense of excitement and expectation as the RSVPs begin to come in. A cookie swap is beautiful when it comes to the range of tastes and types that surface; it's a culinary journey that benefits both the givers and the recipients. Provide a way for people to communicate the recipes or types of cookies they like to prevent duplication. This way, guests can anticipate a mouthwatering range of handcrafted masterpieces and ensure diversity in the cookie assortment.

Provide instructions for how many cookies each person should bring to expedite the process. This keeps there from being an excessive amount of cookies and guarantees that everyone gets a fair portion of the delectable treasure. Generally speaking, each participant should provide twelve cookies for each attendee. This rule achieves a balance by making just enough cookies for everyone to try and take home without going overboard. The location of the cookie swap has a significant impact on how the event goes overall. Think about the mood you want to set, whether it's a virtual exchange, a lively event at a community center, or a small get-together at home. Every location has a certain allure, and the decision is based on the intended mood, the quantity of attendees, and practical factors. While internet swaps enable participation without geographical restrictions and a wider reach, in-person exchanges offer the chance for instant sampling and companionship.

The way the cookies are presented gives the exchange even more charm. Urge participants to use festive plates, ornamental tins, or themed displays to display their cookies attractively. The event becomes a visual and gustatory feast thanks to the visual appeal, which elevates the whole experience. To help participants identify their cookies, think about giving labels or tags that include the recipe name and any pertinent allergy information. This considerate touch makes it easy for guests to choose from the assortment, mainly if there are any dietary requirements or preferences to consider.

Establish a systematic strategy to ensure everyone can taste and gather a share of each cookie to streamline the exchange. A common technique is the round-robin format, in which competitors move between the cookie tables and select a fixed quantity from each set. An alternative would be assigning participants a set sequence to choose the cookies using a numbering system. This guarantees equity and a balanced distribution of the delectable treats. Give participants boxes or containers to bundle their selected cookies, resulting in a lovely assortment they may take home.

The social connections and shared experiences are just as crucial to the success of a cookie exchange as the delicious goodies. Add festive touches to the gathering, like music, decorations, or even a hot chocolate stand, to make it more pleasant. To foster a sense of community and storytelling that gives the event more depth, encourage attendees to discuss the backstories of the dishes they have selected. Consider sharing the cookie exchange a theme, like a particular taste, a fun holiday motif, or an inventive task that fosters friendly competition.

Use technology to create a shared experience for virtual cookie swaps even when participants are physically apart. Participants can remotely interact, converse, and display their cookies via platforms such as video conferencing. Invite guests to dress in holiday attire, tell stories about their experiences baking cookies, and celebrate the season. Consider distributing cookies to attendees ahead of time to preserve the sense of surprise and create an exciting moment of unwrapping and discovery during the virtual event.

A cookie swap is a present that keeps giving because of the happiness it brings to people long after the occasion. Urge attendees to get hard copies of their recipes or submit a digital collection following the occasion. By exchanging recipes, everyone may make versions of their beloved cookies and spread the joy to their circle of friends and family. It turns the cookie exchange into an enduring custom that extends its deliciousness beyond the original get-together.

A photo booth or special place for taking pictures might be included to help preserve the memories of the cookie exchange. Participants may document the experience visually by taking photographs and keeping moments of joy, laughing, and cookie appreciation. To create a virtual book that shares the warmth and camaraderie of the swap with a larger audience, encourage guests to post their images on social media. This preserves the shared moment and maybe a model for further cookie exchanges and celebrations.

As the host, thank the attendees for their participation and the joy they have brought to the occasion. Consider giving modest symbols of thanks, such as recipe cards, holiday cookie cutters, or handwritten thank-you letters. This gesture appreciates each participant's work and excitement for the cookie swap while adding warmth. Beyond just the taste of the food, it creates a lasting impact and strengthens the sense of togetherness.
In summary, throwing a great cookie swap requires a skillful blend of meticulous preparation, considerate planning, and a dash of holiday cheer. Every little detail,

from selecting the ideal location and setting to organizing the cookie exchange smoothly, adds to the overall enchantment of the occasion. The cookie exchange evolves into a celebration of shared experiences, culinary diversity, and inventiveness. The satisfaction of sharing handmade cookies with others, whether in person or digitally, turns the swap into a treasured custom that perfectly encapsulates the spirit of the holidays. The warmth and friendship persist after participants take their carefully chosen assortment of cookies, making the cookie exchange a fun and memorable experience.

Unique Themes for a Memorable Event

In the rich tapestry of Christmas customs, few events are as effective as a cookie exchange party in evoking the warmth and joy associated with the holiday season. Cookie exchanges are more than just the act of exchanging delicious goodies; they are also an occasion to make memories that will last a lifetime, enjoy a variety of flavors, and take pleasure in the inventiveness of people passionate about cooking. To take this cherished custom to new heights, it is necessary to imbue the event with a one-of-a-kind theme that brings an additional dimension of excitement and inventiveness to the proceedings. This essay delves into the fascinating realm of themed cookie exchange parties, revealing a plethora of one-of-a-kind concepts that have the potential to make every get-together an event that is both memorable and delicious.

By participating in a cookie exchange with a traditional theme, you may embrace the enduring allure of the holiday season. Participants should be encouraged to bring traditional Christmas delicacies such as peppermint-flavored delights, sugar cookies decorated with colorful frosting, and gingerbread cookies. Create a festive atmosphere by decorating the location with standard holiday colors, dazzling lights, and seasonal foliage. A warm and inviting ambiance that is reminiscent of cherished traditions is created by this theme, which provides a trip through the delicacies that are most enjoyed throughout the holiday season.

Organizing a cookie exchange with an "Around the World" theme will allow cookie lovers to travel the globe. Make it a requirement for participants to bring cookies influenced by various countries or cultures. The wide variety of sweets, including anything from French madeleines to Italian biscotti, guarantees a flavor-filled voyage. The venue should be decorated with foreign patterns, flags, and ethnic accents to create a joyous and global atmosphere. Not only does this theme honor the uniqueness of the culinary world, but it also provides an experience that is both informative and delectable.

Make the cookie exchange a whimsical winter paradise by transforming it into a beautiful winter wonderland. Sprinkle snowflakes, ice-blue colors, and glittering decorations all over the venue to make it seem festive. For example, you may encourage people to bring cookies flavored with winter tastes, such as spiced snowball cookies or white chocolate cranberry cookies. The participants are invited to taste the delicacy of winter in every mouthful created by this theme, producing a dreamlike and fascinating ambiance.

If you want to add a more involved element to the cookie exchange, arrange a party where people decorate their cookies. Provide cookies in their simple form and various colored icings, sprinkles, and edible embellishments. Participants can express their creative side by decorating cookies on-site or bringing a do-it-yourself kit home. This topic has a hands-on component and converts the exchange into an enjoyable and artistic experience for children and adults passionate about cookies.

When you arrange a cookie exchange with a theme, you may appreciate ugly Christmas sweaters' quirky and joyful spirit. Cookies should be decorated in the style of ugly sweaters, replete with solid patterns, brilliant colors, and festive designs. Participants should be encouraged to contribute cookies made in this style. The occasion will be transformed into a humorous competition by awarding awards to the cookies adorned with the most inventive designs. This lighthearted motif lends a sense of fun and a sense of community to the time-honored ritual of exchanging cookies.

Adding a cocoa and cookies party to the traditional cookie exchange is a great way to take it to the next level. The attendees should be invited to contribute sweets that enhance the chocolate experience, and you should provide a selection of hot cocoa alternatives, ranging from traditional to gourmet flavors. A warm and inviting cocoa bar may be created by combining marshmallows, whipped cream, and flavored syrups. A lovely synergy is created between warm beverages and sweet desserts as a result of this theme, which transforms the exchange into a cozy and gratifying experience.

Attendees will be transported to a bygone historical era through a vintage holiday charm theme. It would help if you encouraged participants to bring cookies based on classic family recipes or dishes from the past. Decorate the location with old holiday ornaments, timeless hues, and touches that evoke nostalgia. Through the use of this subject, an atmosphere of warmth and tradition is created, which is reminiscent of the emotional appeal of times gone by.

Organizing a festive cookie swap and craft party can combine the pleasure of exchanging cookies with the creative satisfaction of making crafts. In addition to participating in holiday-themed handicraft activities, participants can trade cookies. Constructing decorations, wreaths, or personalized cookie packaging can be accomplished by setting up stations for creation. This theme provides the ideal combination of creative and culinary expressions, transforming the event into a multi-sensory and celebratory experience.

A Candyland extravaganza is a great way to add a splash of color and a touch of sweetness to the activity of exchanging cookies. It is recommended that participants bring cookies modeled after traditional candies or that they produce desserts covered with bright colors and whimsical designs. It would help if you decorated the venue with a theme around candy and considered including a candy buffet for the visitors to enjoy. Those passionate about cookies may look forward to a sugary trip with this amusing theme.

A tropical holiday getaway cookie exchange is an excellent opportunity to break away from the usual winter themes that are commonly used. The attendees should be encouraged to contribute cookies infused with tropical tastes such as mango, pineapple, or coconut. Bright colors, tiki torches, and other tropical touches should be used to decorate the venue for the event. The participants will be transported to a paradise drenched in sunshine through the beautiful cookie creations that are a part of this theme, which gives a refreshing spin on holiday traditions.

To summarize, the enchantment of a cookie exchange party is not only in the mouthwatering goodies being exchanged but also in the imaginative and joyous atmosphere being created. The gathering is transformed into a one-of-a-kind and unforgettable occasion with themed cookie exchanges, providing an additional excitement element. Participants will undoubtedly create cherished moments, promote camaraderie, and enjoy the joy of sharing handmade delicacies when they participate in themed cookie exchanges. This is true regardless of whether the participants go on a worldwide culinary voyage or embrace the fantasy of a winter wonderland. Using each subject as a canvas for culinary creativity, cookie fans can demonstrate their abilities while indulging in the holiday season's joyous mood.

Recipes Ideal for Cookie Exchange Parties

A cookie exchange party is made more enjoyable by the variety of flavors and textures each person brings to the table and the fun tradition of exchanging baked cookies. Achieving the ideal cookie exchange recipes requires mixing time-tested favorites, creative inventions, and goodies that hold up well across travel and time. This post looks at a carefully chosen collection of cookie exchange party recipes that combine classic favorites with contemporary tweaks to make the celebration even more delicious and unique.

Classic sugar cookies are a timeless favorite, making a flexible canvas for imaginative decorating and festive forms. Their simplicity lends itself to various variations, from beautifully formed cookies that encapsulate the season's spirit to meticulously decorated masterpieces. A traditional addition to any cookie exchange, classic sugar cookies look great with royal frosting, sprinkles, or a sprinkling of powdered sugar.

Gingerbread cookies are a classic option for the holiday season because of their warm spices and rich molasses flavor. These sweets, whether shaped like traditional gingerbread men, homes, or other festive shapes, bring back fond memories and feelings of coziness. Strong notes of ginger, cinnamon, and cloves are frequently included in the flavor profile, which gives it a rich, warming quality that goes well with hot chocolate or spiced tea.

Meltaway cookies have an excellent peppermint taste, providing a delicious flavor explosion with each mouthful. Coated in powdered sugar, these tiny crumbly cookies are a festive complement to any cookie exchange. They are the perfect option for individuals who value a hint of coolness in addition to the sweetness of the holidays because of their delicate, minty undertones, which create a harmonic balance.

Snickerdoodle cookies are the epitome of cinnamon bliss. The traditional pairing of sugar and cinnamon produces a consistently pleasing sweet and spicy flavor. Snickerdoodles are a big hit at any cookie exchange because of their characteristic broken outside and soft, chewy inside. They stand out among the array of goodies because of their simplicity and mouthwatering flavor.

Chocolate crinkle cookies complement a cookie exchange array with their crackling look and rich chocolaty flavor. The contrast between the dark chocolate inside and the powdered sugar topping produces a striking visual impression. These cookies have a great blend of sweetness and intensity, making them a chocolate lover's dream. They remind me of fudgy brownies.

Linzer cookies are sophisticated and jam-packed, adding something extra to a cookie exchange. The cookie's subtle almond taste goes well with various jams or preserves. These cookies are a visual treat because of their recognizable cutting pattern, which exposes the colorful jam underneath. The fruit filling's nuttiness, sweetness, and faint acidity combine well in these cookies.

Thumbprint cookies, personalized flavor-bursting snacks, are a flexible option for a cookie exchange. Many toppings, such as rich chocolate ganache or fruity jams, are welcome on the tender, buttery foundation. These cookies have a pleasant touch added by the indentation made by a thumb or little spoon, which makes them visually appealing and adaptable to diverse tastes. Almond

flour sugar cookies, which embrace dietary concerns, provide a gluten-free substitute without sacrificing flavor or texture. The cookies still have the traditional qualities of a sugar cookie, but the almond flour adds a subtle nuttiness. These cookies are ideal for meeting various dietary requirements and guarantee that everyone can enjoy the fun of a cookie exchange.

Stained glass cookies are a quirky touch to a cookie exchange since they are edible art pieces. The transparent, colorful sugar cores of these pastries resemble stained glass. Crushed hard candies are inserted into cookie dough cutter parts before baking to provide the desired impression. The end product gives the selection a magical touch and is a gorgeous and visually intriguing treat.

Vegan gingerbread stars, which cater to plant-based diets, provide the comforting, spiced warmth of classic gingerbread without including any animal ingredients. These cookies demonstrate the adaptability of plant-based ingredients, demonstrating that everyone may enjoy tasty snacks. These stars give a lovely scent of warm ginger, cinnamon, and warm cloves for a vegan cookie exchange.

Pecan Sandies, often called Russian tea cakes or Mexican wedding biscuits, are deliciously buttery and nutty treats that melt gently in the mouth. These bite-sized confections, coated in powdered sugar, combine the richness of butter with the crunch of finely chopped nuts. Pecan Sandies, which exemplify simplicity and finesse in every mouthful, lend a touch of luxury to the cookie exchange.

Shortbread cookies, bursting with orange and cranberry flavors, provide a delightfully zesty twist to the classic buttery bliss. The marriage of tart cranberries with tangy orange zest produces a crisp and colorful flavor. Shortbread's crumbly texture gives these cookies a melt-in-your-mouth feel, making them a unique option for anybody looking for a fruity, vibrant blast of flavor.

Mint chocolate chip cookies are a festive twist on the traditional chocolate chip cookie, providing a refreshing, minty touch to the cookie exchange. Chocolate chips and mint essence combine to create a taste combination pleasing to the palate and evocative of a favorite ice cream flavor. These cookies provide a rich and refreshing taste for those who like a touch of mint with their chocolate.

Give classic pecan sandies a taste boost by adding rich, caramelized maple flavor. The pecans' crunch and the maple syrup's warmth combine to create maple pecan sandies, which perfectly embody the spirit of fall. These cookies are elevated by adding maple, which gives them a subtle sweetness that lingers on the tongue and makes them a delicious and cozy treat.

Coconut macaroons are ideal for anyone who enjoys the delicious contrast of sweet and chewy. These cookies have a crisp outside and a soft, chewy inside. They are primarily created with shredded coconut, egg whites, and sugar. Coconut macaroons are a great addition to a cookie exchange since they provide a tropical retreat with every mouthful, whether coated in chocolate or served plain.

To sum up, choosing cookies for a cookie exchange requires careful consideration of dietary restrictions, texture, and flavor. Every dish adds to the entire tapestry of sweet delicacies, from the traditional appeal of sugar cookies to the inventive attraction of stained glass desserts. Whether attendees choose classic favorites or embrace contemporary variations, the cookie exchange transforms into a celebration of creative cooking and good company. These recipes, carefully selected for their allure and adaptability, guarantee to make any cookie exchange a delightful and unforgettable occasion for everybody involved.

CHAPTER VIII

Christmas Cookie Traditions Around the World

Italian Pizzelles: Anise-Flavored Delight

When it comes to classic Italian sweets, pizzelles stand out as a famous and cherished delicacy, and they perfectly reflect the essence of Italy's rich culinary heritage. These waffle-like biscuits, which are thin, fragile, and elaborately designed, have been dazzling palates for ages. They have become a staple in Italian families and a treasured element of cultural festivals. These mouthwatering delights are infused with a distinctive and fragrant character that respects Italy's passion for flavor and tradition. The anise-flavored variant of the pizzelle occupies a unique position among the different variations of the pizza.

Pizzelles may be traced back to the delightful areas of central and southern Italy, where they were first produced using irons heated over an open flame. Pizzelles are known for their thin structure and delicious flavor. Initially, the name "pizzelle" was taken from the Italian word "pizza," which means "round and flat." Pizzelles, traditionally cooked for festive events like weddings, holidays, and family reunions, have become linked with joyful festivities and the warmth of moments spent together.

Pizzelles are characterized by their use of uncomplicated

and timelessly elegant ingredients, which reflect the rustic elegance inherent in Italian cuisine. The foundation of the batter is comprised of flour, eggs, sugar, and butter, which together produce a smooth and flexible composition. It incorporates anise extract or anise seeds into the pizzelle batter. However, that is responsible for imparting the characteristic flavor and scent of the ingredients. The licorice-like tones Anise provides to the cookies lift them to a higher level, providing a sensory experience that is simultaneously reassuring and
stimulating.

When it comes to producing the trademark thinness and crispness of the cookies, preparing the pizzelle batter takes a certain level of finesse because consistency is the key to successful execution. After the batter has been thoroughly combined, a tablespoon is placed in the middle of the pizzelle iron that has been heated. The complex patterns of the iron leave an imprint on the cookie as it cooks, creating a visual tapestry that contributes to the attraction of these delectable treats. As they emerge from the iron, the pizzelles have an anise taste and a golden tint, and their lacy patterns suggest snowflakes or delicate flowers.

During the cooking process of anise-flavored pizzas, the perfume that permeates the kitchen is nothing short of entrancing. The air is filled with Anise's sweet and aromatic notes, which creates an olfactory symphony that heightens the anticipation of the joy that is about to be experienced. It is this sensory experience that displays the creativity and accuracy that are inherent in the making of pizzas. Pizzelles are created by transforming a simple assortment of ingredients into a masterpiece of flavor and tradition.

When it comes to these pizzas, Anise, the show's star, adds more than just its signature flavor to the table. Anise is a spice that is commonly connected with festivals in Italian culture. It is also symbolically associated with good luck and wealth. Pizzelles are enriched with a layer of cultural importance thanks to the inclusion of this ingredient, which not only improves the flavor of the cookies overall but A custom that goes beyond merely being a gastronomic treat is something that families take part in when they meet around the table to enjoy pizzas.
This tradition becomes a connection to the cultural origins, and the stories passed down from generation to generation.

Anise-flavored pizzas are distinguished by their adaptability, one of their distinctive characteristics. Even though these cookies are undoubtedly delicious on their own, they are also an excellent complement to a wide variety of desserts and beverages or even as a garnish. Anise, fragrant and hints of sweetness, is a perfect complement to a shot of liqueur or a cup of espresso. They provide a beautiful balance representing the Italian love for subtle tastes.

In addition to their intrinsic allure, anise-flavored pizzas significantly contribute to the larger cultural fabric of Italian desserts. When it comes to sweets, they join the ranks of biscotti, cannoli, and tiramisu as emblems of Italy's devotion to producing sweets that are not only tasty but also representative of the country's history and the diversity of its regions. The version with anise taste, which pays homage to custom and festivity, demonstrates the skilled artistry and culinary talent characteristic of Italian cuisine.

Even though pizzas are a beloved delicacy throughout the year, they have a particularly significant position in Italian customs during the holidays. During the holiday season, in particular, a plethora of pizzas are placed on tables in homes all across Italy and in Italian communities located all over the world. Producing pizzelles transforms into a joyous ritual, bringing together families to participate in creating and consuming these delectable treats laced with Anise. The entrance of the festive spirit and the joy of being together is signaled by the warm scent of anise-flavored pizzas, which permeates kitchens during this time of year.

Pizzelles with an anise taste have become so popular in modern times that they have crossed cultural borders and captivated people's palates worldwide. Not only are these cookies loved as a sentimental link to Italian ancestry, but they are also cherished as a discovery of new and exquisite tastes. These cookies have found a place in the hearts and homes of individuals who value the art of baking. As a result of the increased demand for pizzelle irons, both traditional and electric, fans are now able to go on their path of producing pizzas, investigating the intricacies of texture and taste.

Pizzelles with an anise taste carry the tales and memories of individuals who have prepared and shared them with others, just like any other culinary heritage. In every mouthful, there is a connection to the hands who painstakingly mixed the batter, the irons that stamped the intricate designs, and the tables where families gathered to relish the results of their labor. Anise-flavored pizzelles encourage people to calm down, appreciate the art of baking, and taste the simple yet profound joys in these delicate biscuits. This is especially important in a world that frequently moves quickly.

In conclusion, anise-flavored pizzelles emerge as an excellent symbol of the junction of flavor, history, and celebration in the background of Italian culinary heritage. Anise-flavored pizzelles reflect the spirit of Italy's passion for making not only food but experiences that go beyond the ordinary. From the smell seduction of Anise to the exquisite patterns etched on each biscuit, anise-flavored puzzles are a perfect example of this dedication. As these cookies make their way onto tables and into hearts, they become ambassadors of a rich cultural legacy that encourages everyone to experience the enchantment of Anise, the artistry of baking, and the joy of gathering together over the shared delight of pizzelles.

German Lebkuchen: Spiced and Iced Perfection

One delicious treat that captures the spirit of the holidays is called Lebkuchen, found deep in Germany's rich culinary heritage. These gingerbread-like biscuits, flavored with spices and icing, have delighted palates for ages. They have gained great respect in German culture and are now a staple of joyous occasions. German Lebkuchen is the pinnacle of culinary artistry and wintertime pleasure, loaded with a harmonic combination of spices, honey, and nuts and topped with a sweet icing frosting.

Lebkuchen's origins are found in the medieval monasteries of Franconia, Germany, where honey and spices in baked items were seen as a sign of refined cuisine. Lebkuchen was formerly a monastery delicacy, but over the ages, it became a popular confection associated with the magical ambiance of Christmas markets and holiday parties all around Germany.

The distinguishing feature of Lebkuchen is its unique spice mixture, known as Lebkuchengewürz. Ground cinnamon, cloves, allspice, nutmeg, and occasionally cardamom are commonly included in this fragrant mixture. The exact ratios of these spices influence the rich and warming taste profile that characterizes Lebkuchen. Lebkuchen is a lovely delicacy that improves with age because the spice combination gives the cookies a powerful scent and a depth of taste that improves daily.

The foundation of Lebkuchen dough is a rich mixture of honey, sugar, eggs, and crushed nuts (almonds, hazelnuts, or walnuts). Not only do these nuts improve the texture, but they also offer a delicate nuttiness that balances the honey's richness. The finished dough is a feat of culinary sorcery that harmoniously combines the powerful warmth of spices and the earthy tones of nuts with sweetness.

The Lebkuchen dough is carefully combined and then let settle for a while to merge and develop the flavors. Usually, the dough is allowed to create for a few days or even weeks, intensifying the flavor's richness. Time is a necessary component in the quest for excellence, and the patience and skill that go into making Lebkuchen are demonstrated by this maturing period.

Lebkuchen shape and baking have a long history of tradition and accuracy. Often, the dough is smoothed out and cut into various forms, such as hearts, stars, rectangles, and rounds. The circular Lebkuchen, which has an embossed image or message and goes back to the 14th century, is a classic design. With carefully designed molds, the elaborate designs are imprinted onto the dough, giving the cookies a little artistic flair.

The kitchen becomes a fragrant haven of warmth and anticipation when Lebkuchen is baked. An aromatic symphony heralding the coming of holiday treats is created as the cookies form in the oven and fill the air with the heavy odors of spices and honey. The cookies are golden in color and have designs engraved on them that tell stories about German culinary history.

But without its crowning glory—the delicious icing frosting that covers its surface—Lebkuchen would be incomplete. Not only does this delightful finish provide a layer of sweetness, but it also provides a blank canvas for artistic decorations. To improve each Lebkuchen's aesthetic appeal, the frosting can be piped in an elaborate design or poured gracefully. Delightful customs are created when bakers decorate Lebkuchen, allowing them to showcase their artistic abilities and personalize these spicy treats.

Lebkuchen's significance in Germany's lively Christmas market culture extends beyond its inherent pleasures. During the Christmas season, these markets, sometimes called Christkindlmarkts, come to life with an enticing assortment of seasonal treats, presents, and, of course, Lebkuchen. Festive decorations around the many forms of Lebkuchen, ranging from the traditional round shapes to the more oversized, heart-shaped pastries bearing romantic inscriptions. The aroma of Lebkuchen permeates the air, bringing the season's charm to life and providing an immersive experience.

Lebkuchen is not limited to just one kind; it manifests itself in a multifaceted mosaic of varieties, each with distinct attributes. For example, Elisenlebkuchen enhances the texture and flavor profile by omitting wheat and using a more significant percentage of nuts. Nürnberger Lebkuchen is a specialty of the city of Nuremberg. It is distinguished by its smaller size, elaborate decorations, and excellent nut-to-wheat ratio. These variants exemplify the geographical diversity and subtleties that add to the depth of the German Lebkuchen heritage.

Beyond being delicious and carefully crafted, Lebkuchen is significant because it represents custom, nostalgia, and group celebration. Lebkuchen making, which brings families together to make and enjoy these spicy delights, traditionally heralds the start of the Christmas season in many German homes. Savoring Lebkuchen becomes an experience for the senses, a link to the past generations who have enjoyed its tastes, and a carrying on of an enduring custom.

Lebkuchen is a dessert typically associated with the Christmas season, but it has transcended cultural barriers and gained a devoted following all year round. Not only does it have holiday connotations, but its warm spices, sweet honey, and nutty richness appeal to all palates. Lebkuchen embodies the spirit of festivity and friendliness in every mouthful, whether consumed with a cup of tea on a calm day or shared with friends during the holidays. Finally, German Lebkuchen is revealed as a masterwork of exquisitely spiced and frosted cake that captures the essence of German holiday customs and the skill of exemplary culinary expertise. Lebkuchen embodies winter pleasure with its fragrant spice combination and delicious balance of nuts and honey. These cookies transcend beyond their culinary form to become a cultural symbol, a link to history, and a lovely representation of the holiday spirit as they make their way into kitchens, festive markets, and the hearts of people who enjoy them.

Mexican Wedding Cookies: A Festive Treat

One delicacy stands out as a sign of joy, warmth, and sweet indulgence among the complex tapestry of culinary traditions associated with Mexico, and that is Mexican Wedding Cookies. These exquisite delicacies, known by various names, such as polvorones or Russian tea cakes, have become a treasured component of weddings, festivals, and get-togethers that are filled with joy. They have been ingrained in the celebratory culture of Mexico. The crumbly texture, nutty richness, and generous sprinkling of powdered sugar characteristic of Mexican Wedding Cookies provide a sensory experience beyond the limitations of taste. These cookies embrace the joy of shared moments and the cultural importance that they assume.

One may trace the origins of Mexican Wedding Cookies back to the culinary influences that originated in the Middle Ages in the Arab world and eventually found their way to Spain. One of the things that the Spanish colonizers brought with them to Mexico was the skill of pastry-making, which included the techniques for manufacturing delicate and crumbly biscuits. These traditions were mixed with local ingredients by Mexican bakers over several centuries, which resulted in a one-of-a-kind hybrid that came to be known as the Mexican Wedding Cookie.

To produce a symphony of tastes, the essential components of Mexican Wedding Cookies are straightforward but precisely blended. Butter, powdered sugar, flour, and crushed nuts are the traditional components of the base. Pecans or walnuts are the nuts of choice for the base. These cookies have a distinctively crumbly texture, resulting from the absence of eggs in the dough component of the recipe. In addition to boosting the sweetness, vanilla extract contributes a delicate aroma that completes the taste profile.

The charm of Mexican Wedding Cookies comes not only in the ingredients that go into making them but also in the mixing process that takes place when the dough is brought together. The buttery richness and crumbly texture are given careful attention to achieve the ideal balance between the two. To make the dough more manageable and straightforward to shape into bite-sized portions, it is frequently refrigerated to stiffen it. The nutty scent is allowed to spread around the kitchen after these rounds are cooked until they have a lovely golden tone.

An extensive coating of powdered sugar is applied to the cookies after removing them from the oven, which is the final step in the transformation process. In addition to giving the cookie a snowy and festive look, this coating also contributes a lovely sweetness that contrasts with the nutty richness of the biscuit. Rolling the warm cookies in powdered sugar becomes a tactile and sensual experience as the sugar sticks to the slightly broken surface. This is because the sugar creates a rich outer layer that cradles the soft inside of the cookies.

Although the term "Mexican Wedding Cookies" may give the impression that these cookies are associated with weddings, it is essential to note that weddings are not the only occasion for which they are consumed. Weddings, quinceañeras, and holiday celebrations are only some of the many happy events ubiquitous in Mexican society. Because of their delicate and endearing character, Mexican Wedding Cookies complement events excellently, emphasizing feelings of sweetness and joy everybody shares.

Mexican Wedding Cookies' adaptability is one factor contributing to their widespread popularity, even beyond the context of cultural events. The ease with which they may be prepared makes them an approachable dessert for home bakers, and several varieties can be found in various cuisines. Snowball cookies or Russian tea cakes are common names for these sweets in the United States, highlighting that they are associated with winter celebrations. The core of these cookies is the same, regardless of the name they go by: they are a delectable bite that encourages a moment of celebration and indulgence if you let it.

Mexican Wedding Cookies are more than just a delectable delicacy; they also have a symbolic importance in Mexican weddings. This is because of the cultural significance that they have. The cookies are regarded as a metaphor for a new marriage's fragile and vulnerable character because of their crumbly texture and delicate appearance. Suppose you want your marriage to be successful. In that case, the powdered sugar symbolizes the sweetness and purity of the union, and the nuts included within the cookie indicate the strength and resilience required for a successful marriage. As these cookies are distributed among the visitors, they transform into not just a delectable culinary treat but also a significant gesture that establishes a connection between the joy of the celebration and the shared cultural traditions.

There is a special place in holiday customs for Mexican Wedding Cookies, particularly during Christmas. Although they are eaten throughout the year, they are most prominent during this time of year. Their look, the spices' warmth, the nuts' richness, and the white aspect all combine to make them an essential component of dessert tables throughout the holiday season. As families celebrate the season's pleasure and relish the richness of these delectable delicacies, preparing and sharing Mexican Wedding Cookies during the holidays becomes a treasured tradition during this time of year.

Mexican Wedding Cookies have made their way into the hearts of dessert lovers worldwide, establishing themselves as a staple in foreign cookies. A delicious texture, a taste profile that strikes a balance between sweetness and the nutty richness of the nuts, and a well-known mix of well-known components all contribute to their widespread appeal. Mexican Wedding Cookies provide comfort and delight that crosses cultural barriers. They can be savored with tea or coffee or as a sweet snack after a meal.

Inviting people to join in the thrill of a treat that reflects the cultural history and the basic pleasures of life, sharing Mexican Wedding Cookies becomes a statement of warmth and hospitality. This is because the cookies are a culturally significant treat. Not only do these cookies become a culinary masterpiece, but they also become a cultural symbol, a tie to tradition, and a joyful representation of the spirit of the holiday season as they make their way into kitchens, celebrations, and moments of shared joy. Each crumbly mouthful of Mexican Wedding Cookies invites folks to experience the sweetness of celebration and the joy of coming together around the shared delight of these festive goodies. These cookies perfectly exemplify how Mexican wedding cookies can bring people together.

CHAPTER IX

Troubleshooting and FAQs

Common Cookie Baking Problems and Solutions

For those who bake at home, the craft of cookie baking may bring them joy and occasionally irritation with its beautiful scents and sweet rewards. The prospect of warm, freshly made cookies is alluring, but getting there can be challenging. Whether seasoned pros or beginners, many bakers have similar problems that might compromise the quality of their baked goods. Every baking issue, from uneven browning to flat cookies, offers a chance to improve one's technique. We dig into the subtleties of the baking process in this examination of typical cookie-baking issues and their fixes, providing insights to assist bakers in troubleshooting and producing the ideal batch of cookies.

Overly spreading cookies might be one of the most frequent problems bakers encounter; this can leave the cookies looking thin and flat. Frequently, too-warm or too-softened butter is the issue. Ensure your butter is at the right temperature—softened but still chilly to the touch—to fix this. To further assist in firming the fats in the dough and minimize excessive spreading, chill the cookie dough for a little while before baking. Using the proper flour ratio to leavening agents, too flat cookies may result from too much baking soda or too little flour. You may achieve a thicker, more satisfying cookie by experimenting with dough cooling periods and adjusting these elements.

One typical complaint is a crumbly and dry texture, usually caused by an uneven amount of moist to dry components. Since overmixing activates the gluten in the wheat, overmixing the cookie dough can also result in a dry texture. To solve this problem, measure your components carefully and add your dry ingredients only until they are incorporated, being cautious not to overmix. Extra egg yolk or a little milk can provide moisture to the dough, improving texture without sacrificing taste.

Inadequate cookie positioning on the baking sheet or inconsistent oven temperatures can lead to uneven browning. Invest in an oven thermometer to check the precision of your oven's temperature and guarantee uniform browning. Halfway through the baking process, turn the baking sheets to ensure that they receive equal heat exposure. When cookies are arranged too closely on a sheet, air circulation around them becomes hindered, which can also lead to uneven browning. Enough distance between cookies facilitates even baking and a steady golden color.

If you add chocolate chips, almonds, or other mix-ins to the cookie dough, the additions may be concentrated in one part of the cookie rather than distributed evenly. To avoid this, consider manually adding mix-ins to the cookie dough balls before baking. In addition to ensuring a more even distribution, this stops certain cookies from being overstuffed with sweets while others stay simple. Alternatively, you may improve the appearance of the cookies by setting aside some of the mix-ins to press onto the tops right before baking.

Finding the ideal sweetness level is a personal choice that might vary depending on personal tastes. However, by carefully measuring sugar amounts and experimenting with the sugar used, one may change an output that is either too sweet or not sweet enough. Granulated sugar gives sweetness and structure, while dark brown sugar adds moisture and a deep molasses taste. By adjusting the kinds and quantities of sugar, bakers may precisely control the sweetness of their cookies to suit individual tastes.

Too much butter or shortening in the dough might cause cookies to have too oily bottoms. Adding a little more flour or lowering the fat level will aid in absorbing extra grease when baking. To limit direct contact between the dough and the surface and lessen the possibility of greasy bottoms, use parchment paper or a silicone baking mat on the cookie sheets.

With the proper lubrication or parchment paper, you can lessen the annoyance of cookies sticking to the baking pan. To make a non-stick surface, ensure the baking sheet is well-greased or coated with parchment. Using parchment paper makes removing the cookies off the sheet easy and avoids any possible sticking. Another way to reduce the likelihood of cookies sticking is to let them cool on the baking sheet for a few minutes before moving them to a cooling rack.

When cookies are overmixed, the gluten in the flour is activated, and the texture becomes rough or rubbery. Mix the ingredients until incorporated, being careful not to whisk too much to prevent this. Another way to get a soft texture is to use flour with less protein, such as cake flour. Another way to make cookies more peaceful and pleasurable is to ensure the butter isn't too softened and add enough fat.
There are a few reasons cookies could crack on the outside, including using too much flour or leavening

chemicals. Be careful to measure the dry ingredients precisely, and experiment with a little less flour. The cookie batter should be well chilled before baking for a smoother surface. Surface cracks can also be minimized by gently forming the cookie dough into balls and letting some natural spreading occur while baking.

There might be a few reasons cookies don't spread out when baking and keep their mound-like structure. A lack of spread might be caused by too much flour, too little fat, or too cold dough. Make sure the butter is softened enough, and if necessary, modify the amount of flour to get the right consistency. Let the cookie dough come to room temperature before baking to encourage the ideal spread while baking.

In conclusion, mastering the subtleties of baking and realizing how different elements affect the finished product are essential steps to making the ideal cookies. Even though frequent baking issues with cookies might occur, each one offers a chance for growth and development. Equipped with this information, bakers may experiment, solve problems, and set out on a delectable mission to become experts in cookie creation. In addition to being a culinary achievement, baking cookies perfectly and freshly is a source of great happiness for the baker who shares these delicious delights with others.

Frequently Asked Questions About Christmas Cookies

Every kitchen in the globe is filled with the delightful scent of freshly baked Christmas cookies as the holiday season draws near. These delicious delicacies are more than just candies; they are an essential part of holiday customs that unite families and fill homes with the coziness and cheer of the season. Nevertheless, even the most seasoned bakers might find themselves wondering about various topics about the craft of making Christmas cookies. This examination of often-asked concerns regarding Christmas cookies delves into the subtleties of ingredients, methods, and age-old customs that contribute to these delicacies' status as a treasured holiday delicacy.

Is it Possible to Freeze Cookie Dough in Advance?

A frequently asked question by time-pressed bakers is whether cookie dough may be frozen ahead of time. Without a doubt, the answer is yes. Preparing ahead of time is made more accessible and more convenient using frozen cookie dough. Once the dough is well combined, divide it into parts or roll it into logs. Tightly wrap the dough in plastic and store it in a freezer-safe bag. Just defrost the dough in the fridge or at room temperature and continue baking when ready to bake. This method not only makes baking more accessible but also guarantees that fresh-made cookies are always available throughout the busy Christmas season.

How Do I Get the Optimal Texture in My Cookies?

Understanding important variables and paying attention to detail is necessary for the ideal cookie texture. It is essential to balance the amount of moist and dry materials. You may change the texture by experimenting with the proportions of components like flour, sugar, and fat. An additional egg yolk and a more significant proportion of brown sugar to granulated sugar provide moisture and suppleness to chewy cookies. On the other hand, cookies with a more extensive granular sugar content have a crisp texture and are golden and snappy.

What Characterizes Soft and Chewy Cookies?

Mixing ingredients and processes is required to achieve the sought texture of soft and chewy cookies, a perennial favorite. Brown sugar gives cookies their suppleness because of its increased moisture content and molasses taste. Adding cornstarch to the dry ingredients results in a more delicate texture, and underbaking the cookies just a little bit keeps them chewy. Furthermore, the type of fat used, such as butter or shortening, influences the texture overall. Butter adds a deep taste, while shortening improves softness.

Are Ingredients in Cookie Recipes Replaceable?

Because cookie recipes are so flexible, you can change the ingredients to suit your dietary needs or pantry. For instance, vegetable oil or margarine can frequently be used instead of butter; however, the flavor and texture may differ. Similarly, applesauce, yogurt, or flaxseed can be used instead of eggs for individuals who prefer eggless options. However, it's essential to consider each ingredient's unique function in the recipe and foresee how different alternatives can affect the outcome.

How Can I Stop Cookies from Excessively Spreading?

Excessive spreading is a typical worry for bakers who want their cookies to be precisely formed. Ensuring the butter is at the right temperature—softened but not too so—will assist in limiting spreading to remedy this problem. Chilling the cookie dough before baking is also beneficial, as this helps decrease spread and solidify the fats. You may further refine the form of the cookie and avoid unintended thinness by experimenting with different leavening agents and adjusting the flour-to-fat ratio.

What Intriguing Christmas Cookie Decorating Ideas Exist?

Christmas cookies offer a platform for artistic expression and festivity. Beyond frosting and sprinkles, bakers have many decorating options at their disposal. Because of its glossy, smooth appearance, royal icing is perfect for detailed patterns and decorations. Present presentations may be colorful and artistic, thanks to edible paints and food coloring gels. A distinctive touch may be added with cookie stamps, molds, and embossing tools. Depth and visual interest can be created by stacking several types of icing. Christmas cookie decorating becomes an artistic undertaking, encouraging bakers to use their creativity to create tasty works of art that bring holiday pleasure.

How Do I Guarantee Proper Baking?

A batch of cookies that are consistently tasty requires even baking. Even outcomes are influenced by precise oven temperature, positioning cookies on baking pans, and rotating them throughout the baking process. Purchasing an oven thermometer guarantees accurate temperature settings. Enough air circulation is made possible by adequately spacing cookies on baking sheets, which helps to avoid uneven baking—rotating the baking sheets halfway through guarantees that every cookie is exposed to the same heat, producing a consistent, golden finish.

What Christmas Cookie Substitutes Are Gluten-Free?

As dietary preferences and limits become more widely known, many bakers seek gluten-free substitutes for Christmas cookies. Popular alternatives to regular wheat flour include almond flour, coconut flour, and gluten-free all-purpose flour. These substitutes not only accommodate those who are intolerant to gluten but also give the cookies new tastes and sensations. Creating sweets that are inclusive and accessible to a wide range of flavors may be achieved by experimenting with gluten-free recipes.

Can I Bake Christmas Cookies Without Eggs?

Making vegan Christmas cookies is substituting plant-based components for conventional animal-based ones. Vegan margarine or coconut oil can be used instead of butter, while applesauce, mashed bananas, or flaxseed diluted with water can replace eggs. Vegan chocolate chips and nondairy milk are cruelty-free choices. By modifying recipes to suit vegan tastes, bakers may share holiday delicacies with people who follow plant-based diets, unleashing creative possibilities.

How Should Christmas Cookies Be Stored to Preserve Their Freshness?
To keep Christmas cookies fresh and high-quality, proper storage is essential. After the cookies are cooked and completely cool, store them in airtight containers to keep moisture and air out. Maintaining distinct tastes can be supported by dividing different cookie kinds with parchment or wax paper layers. Cookies may be frozen in either raw dough or cooked form for extended storage. To enjoy, merely defrost frozen cookies at room temperature or reheat them for a little while in the oven to achieve a freshly baked flavor.
In summary, the world of Christmas cookies is just as big and varied as the customs surrounding the holidays. Understanding the complexities of cookie-making calls for ingenuity, experimentation, and a readiness to adjust to different dietary requirements and tastes. Scooping out the ideal texture, experimenting with other ingredients,

or perfecting the decorating technique is just as satisfying as the finished sugary morsels. These commonly asked questions guide bakers as they set out on the festive adventure of preparing Christmas cookies, inspiring a joyous exploration of the delectable possibilities that make the holiday season genuinely unique.

CONCLUSION

As we end the enjoyable voyage through the pages of "Unveiling the Magic of Christmas Cookies: Seasonal Sweets Unveiled - An Introduction to Christmas Cookies," we find ourselves completely submerged in the fantastical world of holiday baking. This electronic book has been a travel companion, assisting bakers of all expertise levels, from novices to seasoned professionals, in navigating the artistic and joyful process of making Christmas cookies. The e-book has acted as a thorough guide to fill the holiday season with the sweet enchantment of handmade goodies. It has covered everything from learning the fundamental methods of cookie dough to exploring the varied flavors and textures of renowned recipes.

As we bid farewell this e-book, we are left with a treasure trove of knowledge to draw upon. It has equipped readers with the essential information to embark on a smooth baking journey, exploring crucial baking tools and ingredients. Each chapter has unveiled the secrets behind some of the most beloved Christmas treats, from sugar cookies' timeless allure to gingerbread's aromatic warmth and the playful delight of stained glass cookies.
Beyond just recipes, the e-book delved into the finer aspects of successful cookie baking. It addressed common challenges, offered creative decorating tips, and catered to various dietary needs. More than just a guide, it fostered creativity and encouraged personal touches in each batch of cookies, designed to meet bakers' diverse needs and aspirations.

While we are contemplating the voyage through the chapters, we are reminded that the enchantment of

Christmas cookies goes much beyond the components that are mentioned in a recipe. It lies in the memories that are built when baking with loved ones, the delight that comes from sharing freshly baked goods with friends and neighbors, and the warmth that stays in the heart with each festive taste.

An invitation is extended in the form of "Unveiling the Magic of Christmas Cookies" to enter the kitchen with self-assurance, embrace the joy of creation, and appreciate the time-honored tradition of Christmas cookie enchantment. This e-book has shed light on the path that leads to a season filled with sweetness, warmth, and the unmistakable magic of Christmas. Whether it's the nostalgic aroma wafting through the house, the laughter shared during a cookie decorating session, or the joy of gifting a beautifully packaged box of homemade delights, this e-book has illuminated the path.

Thank you for buying and reading/listening to our book. If you found this book useful/helpful please take a few minutes and leave a review on the platform where you purchased our book. Your feedback matters greatly to us.